Adorable
Pom Pom Animals
Dogs, Cats and Other Woolly Friends

KAZUKO ITO

TUTTLE Publishing

Tokyo | Rutland, Vermont | Singapore

Contents

Introduction

When I was in the first grade, my mother bought me a book. It was a craft book with instructions for making little animals. That book made my heart sing, and I made many animals. Even now, I can still vividly remember that joyful feeling.

Time has passed, and I am still making handmade goods with that same joy. Sometimes I experience the challenges that come with creating something new, but the feeling that comes with surmounting the issues and watching the projects take form is unbeatable.

In this book, I introduce pom pom projects suitable for all levels: from absolute beginners to more advanced crafters. While making these projects, I hope that you too will feel the kind of joy I discovered as a first-grader and beyond. Welcome to the wonderful world of pom poms!

Kazuko Ito

Rabbit

An adorable bunny with droopy ears
made out of fluffy felted wool.

instructions > page 46

Sheep

This cuddly sheep with soft, fuzzy fleece balances on felted wool feet.

instructions > page 56

Poodle

A pair of irresistible eyes characterize this little pom pom pup. The yarn creates the perfect poodle fur texture.

instructions > page 57

Miniature Schnauzer

Those eyebrows and snout!
Felted wool ears add just the right touch.

instructions > page 58

Calico Cat

Create this multi-colored kitty with three colors of yarn. The pink nose makes for a dose of added cuteness.

instructions > page 60

Brown Tiger Cat

With its distinctive stripes, this brown
tiger cat has extra pointy ears.

instructions > page 60

Bear

Increase the cuteness factor by placing the eyes and nose close together.

instructions > page 59

Lion

This handsome creature sports piercing
eyes and a regal, luxurious mane.

instructions > page 62

Monkey

Keeping the size of the eyes
small gives this monkey a more
sophisticated appearance.

instructions > page 63

Elephant

A pipe cleaner inside the trunk
allows this elephant's nose to be
positioned in different ways.

instructions > page 64

Cat

This endearing fluffy cat is made all the more so by its pink ears.

instructions > page 65

Dachshund

How can you resist its sparkly eyes
gazing up at you from its cocked head?

instructions > page 66

Penguin

Even the back of this roly-poly penguin,
is like a delightful little kid.

instructions > page 67

Seal

A seal is perfect for a pom pom! Ratchet up the cuteness factor with big black eyes.

instructions > page 68

Tropical Fish

Trim the pom pom to produce a
trim tropical fish-like silhouette.

instructions > page 69

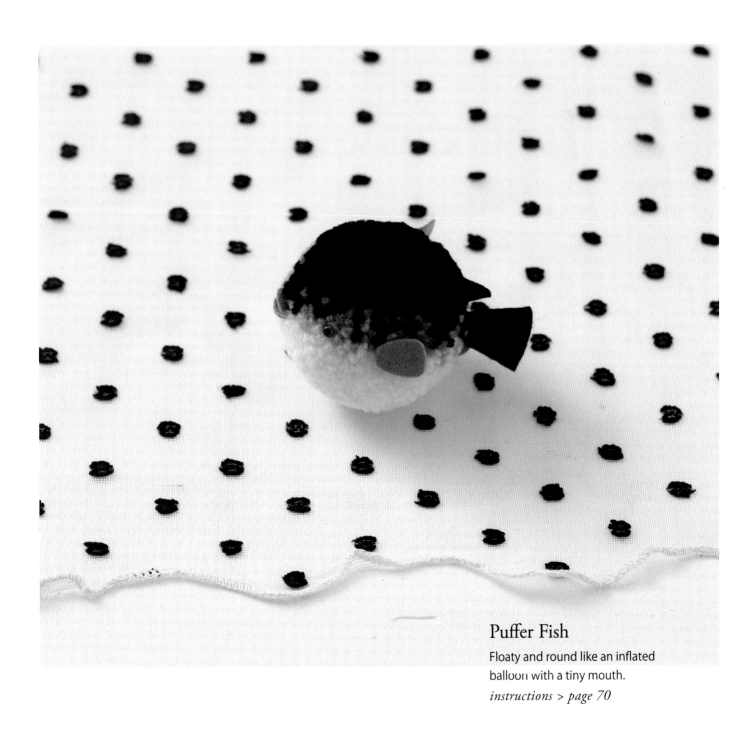

Puffer Fish

Floaty and round like an inflated balloon with a tiny mouth.

instructions > page 70

Parakeet

Charming parakeets are even
sweeter in multiples, lined up.

instructions > page 71

Frog

This winsome froggy has eyes full of curiosity and an itty bitty nose.

instructions > page 72

Pig

Squeal-worthy cuteness standing on four legs,
especially its backside with the curly tail.

instructions > page 73

Strawberry Bunny

It's hard to get cuter than this: a pointy-eared rabbit tuft wearing a strawberry hat.

instructions > page 74

Hamster

You could even add a little flower
bouquet to its sweetly poised limbs.

instructions > page 75

Chick

The downiness and size of this pom pom
chick feel almost like the real thing.

instructions > page 76

Hamburger Set

【 Hamburger, Broccoli, Boiled Egg, Cherries 】
Assembled in a basket. The pom pom hamburger is
almost as large as a real burger.

instructions >
page 77 (Hamburger), page 78 (Broccoli),
page 79 (Cherry), page 82 (Boiled Egg)

Onigiri Rice Ball Set

【 2 Types of Onigiri, Fried Shrimp, Sausage, Broccoli, Apple 】
The "bento box" Is full of yummy side dishes.

instructions >
page 80 (2 types of Onigiri), page 78 (Broccoli),
page 79 (Apple), page 80 (Sausage),
page 81 (Fried Shrimp)

Round Cake

A lovely mini-round cake with 2 shades
of cream filling. Add a cherry on top.

instructions > page 83

Cupcakes

The whipped cream looks delicious!
The final flourish is the strawberry on top.

instructions > page 84

Ice Cream Cones

Single and double scoop ice cream cones in sweet pastel yarn pom poms.

instructions > page 85

Apple Pencil Topper

A pencil is always more fun with a pom pom apple on top of it.

instructions > page 86

Seasonal Pom Poms

How about celebrating seasonal events with pom poms? Simply place a few on your windowsill or on a shelf to create instant festivity. Insert a string through the center of the pom pom and hang several of them like a mobile!

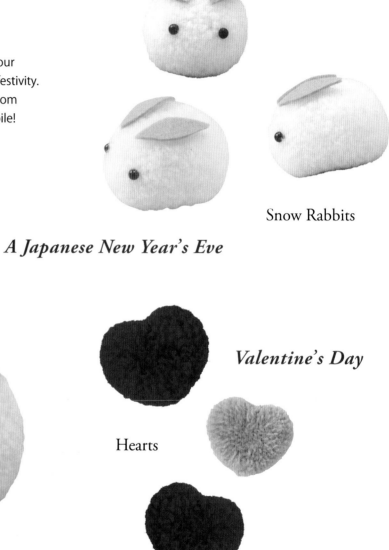

Snow Rabbits

A Japanese New Year's Eve

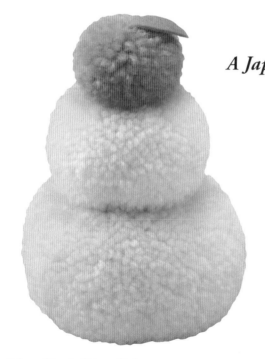

New Year's Rice Cakes
(Kagami Mochi)

Valentine's Day

Hearts

Spring

Flower A

Flower B

Two Types of Flowers

Autumn

Halloween Pumpkins

instructions >
Kagami Mochi > page 87
Two Types of Flowers > page 88
Snow Rabbit > page 89
Heart > page 89
Halloween Pumpkin > page 90

Tools | Basic tools used in this book

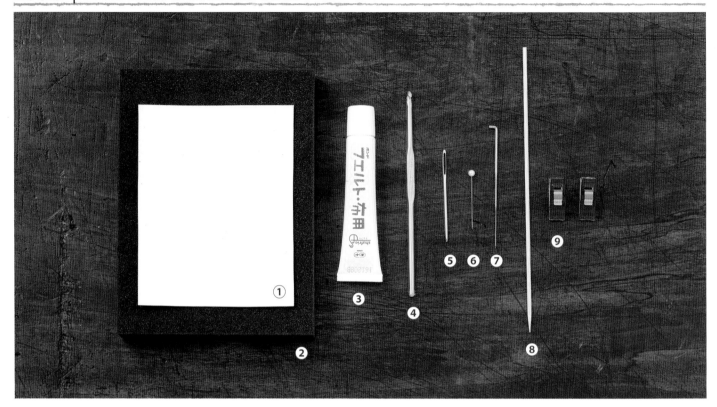

① Cardboard
For making ears and mini pom poms. Also useful for felting small amounts of wool roving since the cardboard prevents accidental stabbing of fingers.

② Felting Needle Mat
Place this mat beneath the wool roving to use felting needles.

③ Fabric or Craft Glue
Dab to secure knots when attaching strings or to adhere eyes, ears and legs to pom poms.

④ Crochet Hook
Use to connect pom poms together. With larger pom poms, a yarn darning needle may not be long enough so a crochet hook is handy to have.

⑤ Yarn Darning Needle
For connecting ears to the head and such. Select a needle with an eye that will accommodate the thickest string or yarn you will be using.

⑥ Pins
To indicate eyes and nose positions or to mark the crown of the head when trimming the pom pom.

⑦ Felting Needle
For felting wool roving. Also used to attach ears, nose and legs to pom poms (we will refer to it as simply "needle" in this book).

⑧ Bamboo Stick
Helpful for adding small drops of glue to beads and string knots.

⑨ Clips
Secure various sections with clips while felt pieces are drying once glue has been applied to form shapes. Clothespins work as well. Small sizes are recommended.

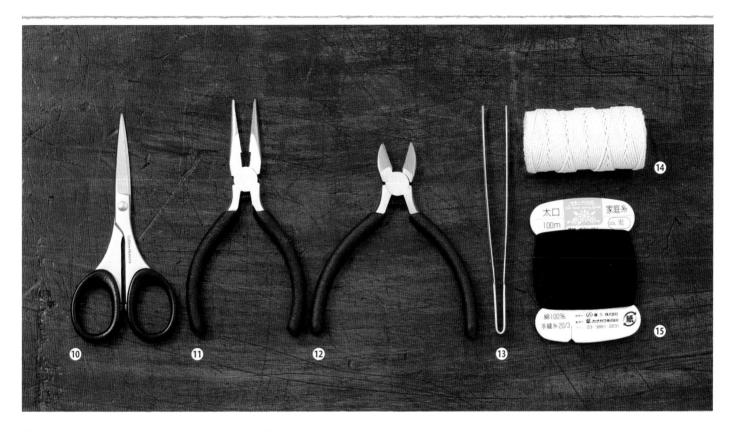

⑩ Scissors
Try to use scissors with extra sharp tips. It should fit comfortably in your hand.

⑪ Round Nose Pliers
Pliers with rounded tips. Use to bend wires.

⑫ Wire Cutter
For cutting wire and to trim eyes and nose parts that may be too long.

⑬ Tweezers
To arrange and adjust pom pom yarn during construction. It's also helpful for picking up small parts such as beads and eyes.

⑭ String or Twine
Use to tie the center of the pom pom. We recommend kite string.

⑮ Heavy Duty Sewing Thread
For tying the center of mini-pom poms or to create the mouth for some of the animals.

Pom Pom Sizing

Below are the different sizes of pom pom makers and the corresponding pom poms for reference. Pom pom density will vary depending on the thickness of the yarn and the number of times the yarn is wound; some will be thick and solid, while others may be fluffier and soft.

※The two arms are combined and the yarn is wound on each half.
Instructions will indicate which side to wind first with A. B will be wound next.

※The pom pom maker used for the projects in these books was Hamanaka Kuru Kuru Pom Pom Maker, a Japanese brand. Many different brands are available, such as Clover, Lion and others. Sizes, design and instructions for use vary from brand to brand, so it's a good idea to visit craft shops for a good look, and check out YouTube videos to see how they're used. Buying a set is a good idea too, so that the different sizes will be in proportion with one another.

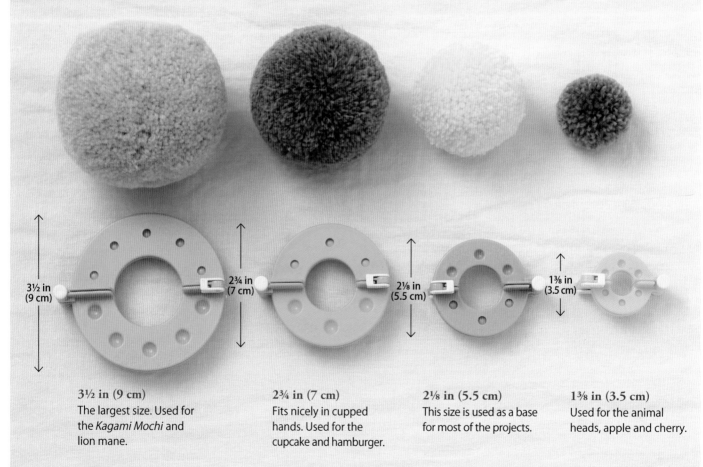

3½ in (9 cm)

2¾ in (7 cm)

2⅛ in (5.5 cm)

1⅜ in (3.5 cm)

3½ in (9 cm)
The largest size. Used for the *Kagami Mochi* and lion mane.

2¾ in (7 cm)
Fits nicely in cupped hands. Used for the cupcake and hamburger.

2⅛ in (5.5 cm)
This size is used as a base for most of the projects.

1⅜ in (3.5 cm)
Used for the animal heads, apple and cherry.

Yarns

Select the appropriate yarns. The photo below is a guide to the weights that are most commonly used in these projects. If you prefer a different yarn, or the recommended types aren't available to you, adjust for differing weight by increasing the number of windings for thinner yarn and vice versa.

※ Actual size shown in photo

A Pom Pom Yarn (sport weight)

B Machine Washable Sport Weight

C Worsted Weight

D Machine Washable Merino
   (worsted weight)

E Alpaca Merino
   (worsted weight)

F Mohair (sport weight)

G Curly Mohair
   (super bulky weight)

H Bulky Weight

Taking up the yarn ends
To wind two strands at once, take one strand from the outer part of the yarn ball or skein, and another strand from the inside; if you insert your fingers into the center of the ball, you should find a clump of yarn that can be pulled out.

Other Materials

Supplies needed in addition to yarn for project construction.
For felt and wool roving, try to find similar materials.

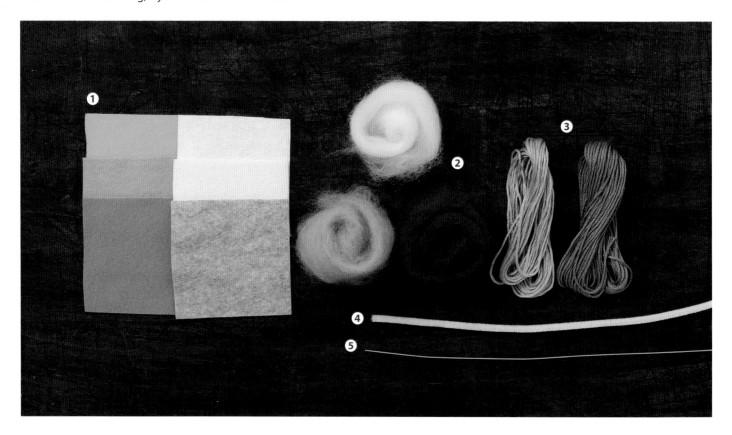

① Felt
Used for the hamster and cat ears, the penguin's beak, etc. A thin layer of craft glue is applied on both sides of the felt. Once the glue is dry, cutting out small pieces is a snap.

② Wool Roving
Ears, nose, legs are formed by felting wool roving with a special felting needle on top of a felting needle mat.
※ We use the "Flufeel" brand roving in this book.

③ Embroidery Floss Size 25
Create the chick's legs by wrapping the embroidery floss around a piece of wire.

④ Pipe Cleaner
By wrapping wool roving around the pipe cleaner and using a needle to felt it, the elephant's nose and cat's tail can be shaped.

⑤ Wire
For the chick's leg and fried shrimp.

Eyes • Noses Parts

The eyes and nose pieces are essential in creating facial expressions. We've listed a variety of sizes, shapes and colors of plastic safety eyes and noses below. Slight modifications to the eye placement can completely alter the expression, so play around with different arrangements (see p. 54).

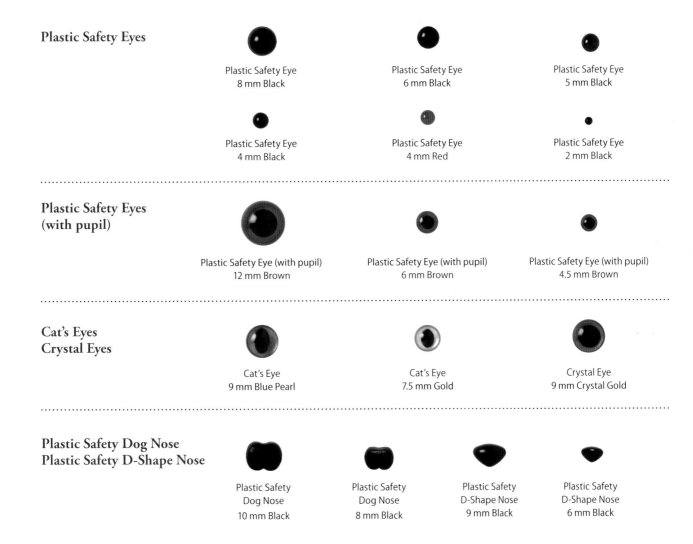

Plastic Safety Eyes

Plastic Safety Eye
8 mm Black

Plastic Safety Eye
6 mm Black

Plastic Safety Eye
5 mm Black

Plastic Safety Eye
4 mm Black

Plastic Safety Eye
4 mm Red

Plastic Safety Eye
2 mm Black

Plastic Safety Eyes (with pupil)

Plastic Safety Eye (with pupil)
12 mm Brown

Plastic Safety Eye (with pupil)
6 mm Brown

Plastic Safety Eye (with pupil)
4.5 mm Brown

Cat's Eyes Crystal Eyes

Cat's Eye
9 mm Blue Pearl

Cat's Eye
7.5 mm Gold

Crystal Eye
9 mm Crystal Gold

Plastic Safety Dog Nose Plastic Safety D-Shape Nose

Plastic Safety
Dog Nose
10 mm Black

Plastic Safety
Dog Nose
8 mm Black

Plastic Safety
D-Shape Nose
9 mm Black

Plastic Safety
D-Shape Nose
6 mm Black

※ Actual size shown in photo

Pom Pom Basics ①

Let's Make a Chick Hair Tie
(Template on page 45)

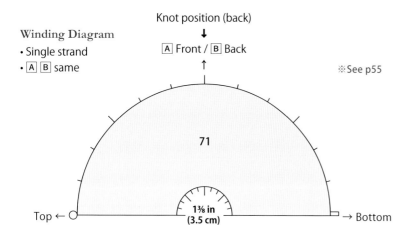

Winding Diagram
- Single strand
- A B same

Knot position (back)

A Front / B Back

※See p55

71

Top ← O

1⅜ in
(3.5 cm)

→ Bottom

> ### Materials
>
> Pom pom maker: 1⅜ in (3.5 cm)
> Yarn – worsted weight in lemon
>
> **Other Materials**
> Eyes: plastic safety eye (black) 4 mm x 2
> Beak: felt (orange) 1 x 1 in (2.5 x 2.5 cm)
> Backing: felt (black) 1⅝ x 1⅝ in (4 x 4 cm)
> Hair tie elastic: approximately 8 in (20 cm)

Trimming and Sizing Guide

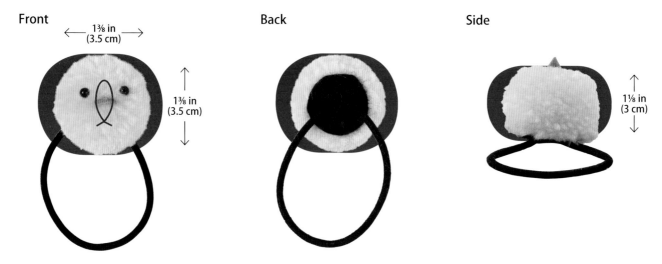

Front
← 1⅜ in →
(3.5 cm)
1⅜ in
(3.5 cm)

Back

Side
1⅛ in
(3 cm)

Instructions

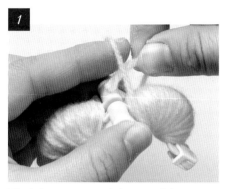

Wind the yarn around the arm of the pom pom maker 71 times, going back and forth across the arm (indicated by A on the diagram). Once the winding is complete, loop the yarn around your index finger once, leave a tail of about 2 in (5 cm) and cut. Insert the end of the yarn into the loop around your finger and tighten. Repeat on the opposite side (indicated as B).

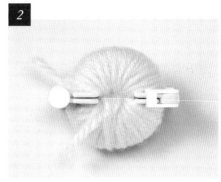

If it becomes difficult to wrap the yarn around the other arm, keep winding in the center of the arm instead of going back and forth.

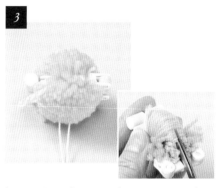

Insert scissors between the two arms and cut the yarn all around. In the groove formed, loop a string (such as kite string) twice, tighten and knot securely at the position indicated on the diagram.

Open the arms and take out the pom pom. Using the trimming and sizing visual guide, trim the pom pom.

Don't worry about precision at first and snip the pom pom into the general shape desired.

Once you have the approximate shape, carefully trim every part of the pom pom uniformly.

Let's Make a Chick Hair Tie (continued)

Trimmed.

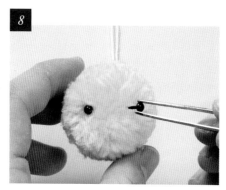

Figure out the eye placement and glue into place.

Take the orange felt for the beak and apply a thin layer of glue on one side. Fold in half, glued side together.

Once dry, use the template and cut out the beak shape.

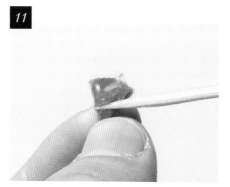

Apply a thin layer of glue on the top of the beak with a bamboo stick and let dry. Repeat with the other side of the beak.

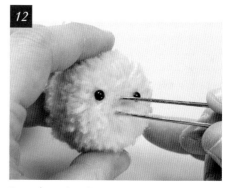

Determine the placement of the beak. Use tweezers to separate the yarn where the beak will be placed.

13

Glue the beak in place. Rearrange the yarn around the beak and let the glue dry.

14

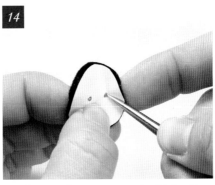

Use the template to cut out the felt backing. Keeping the template on the backing, create the two holes with an awl. Then thread the elastic ends through the holes and tie together.

15

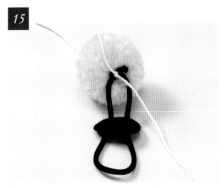

Tie pom pom string to the elastic.

16

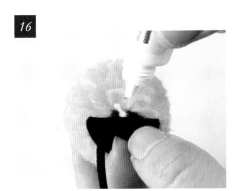

Snip the end of the string as close to the knot as possible and apply glue. Pull the felt backing up to the base of the pom pom. Apply glue to half of the backing and attach to pom pom. Repeat with the other half of backing.

Complete!

Template (actual size)

Felt Backing

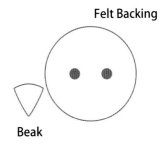

Beak

Pom Pom Basics ②

Rabbit (see page 6)
(Template on page 93)

Winding Diagram
- Double strand
- A B same

Knot position (back)
↓
A Front / B Back

※See p55

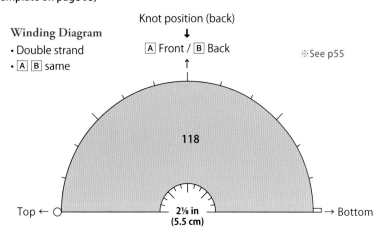

118

Top ← ○
2⅛ in
(5.5 cm)
→ Bottom

Materials

Pom pom maker: 2⅛ in (5.5 cm)
Yarn – alpaca merino in camel

Other Materials
Eyes: plastic safety eye (black) 8 mm x 2
Ear: wool roving (light tan/biscuit color)
Nose: felt (dark brown) ⅞ x ⅞ in (2 x 2 cm)

Trimming and Sizing Guide

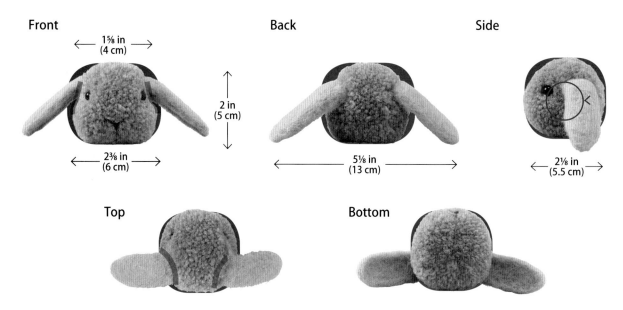

Front

1⅝ in
(4 cm)

2 in
(5 cm)

2⅜ in
(6 cm)

Back

5⅛ in
(13 cm)

Side

2⅛ in
(5.5 cm)

Top

Bottom

Instructions

1

Follow the winding diagram and wrap the yarn 118 times to make a 2⅛ in (5.5 cm) pom pom. For how to make a pom pom, refer to the Chick Hair Tie steps 1–4 (p.43).

2

Shape into a triangular shape with loose, rough cuts.

3

Roughly-formed shape.

4

Determine eye placement and separate yarn with tweezers to insert the eye pieces. Do not glue yet.

5

If the eye or nose fastener is too long, cut down to desired length with pliers.

6

Insert eyes as deeply as possible. If you have to adjust the eye position, fix the yarn with tweezers before re-inserting.

Rabbit (continued)

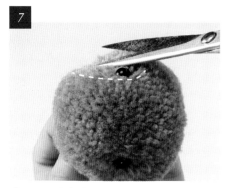

7

Flatten and slightly hollow out the section from above the eye to the top of the head (dotted line in photo) and round out the shape from below the eye.

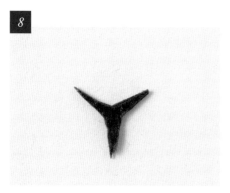

8

Apply glue to the felt with a bamboo stick and let dry. Once dry, use the template to cut out the nose shape.

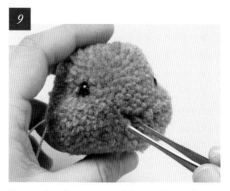

9

Determine the nose position and attach with glue.

10

Glue eyes into positions determined from step 4.

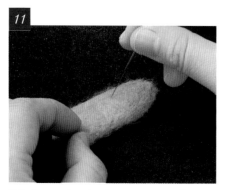

11

Felt the wool roving into ears using the template.

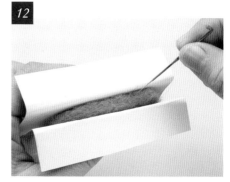

12

Once the ears are felted into the desired shape, place between cardboard pieces and felt the sides as well. This helps you form the shape easily while avoiding injury.

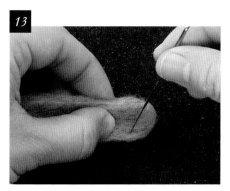

13

Pinch with your thumb to curve the bottom of the ear and felt with the needle. Felt the upper tip of the ear as well.

14

Use pins to determine ear position.

15

Separate the yarn at the base of the pins with tweezers.

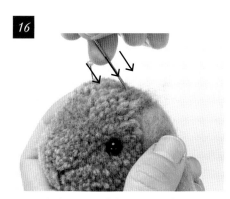

16

Insert the bottom of the ear into the pom pom and stab into place with the felting needle. Rearrange the yarn around the ear to blend it in.

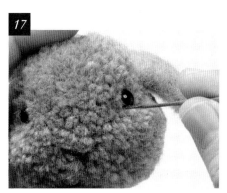

17

Lightly felt the area above the eye with the needle to give it some pointy texture.

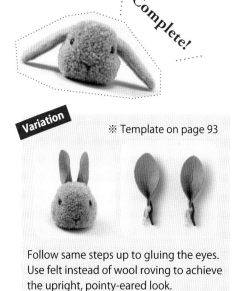

Complete!

Variation   ※ Template on page 93

Follow same steps up to gluing the eyes. Use felt instead of wool roving to achieve the upright, pointy-eared look.

Basic Tips

These tips will ensure a well-made pom pom.

Adjusting the flow of yarn

Once removed from the pom pom maker, use tools such as tweezers to rearrange the yarn for even distribution. In cases when two or more colors are part of the pom pom, adjust areas where colors have gotten mixed up before trimming for cleaner results.

Cut strings at the base

When tying the pom pom at the center, make sure the string isn't visible by knotting as tightly as possible and cutting the string ends close to the base of the knot. By securely wrapping and tying the string, you may not need to use glue.

Using Pins

Some pom poms call for color changes or require switching tasks while still in winding mode. Insert pins to secure the yarn when you have to release the pom pom maker.

Trimming Methods

The following introduces a variety of trimming methods.

Stepped Cut

Finish Cut

1 To add a stepped cut in places where two colors meet, for example, press down and separate the section you want to cut with scissors.

2 Tilt and lay the scissors from step 1 to the side that will be shorter and trim (used for the cupcake and strawberry bunny).

Trim carefully, practically snipping each yarn piece. This produces a smooth finish.

Pom Pom Techniques ②

How to Make a Mini Pom Pom

Great for ears, muzzles and small sizes not doable with a pom pom maker. Cardboard is used.

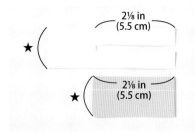

1 Prepare two pieces of cardboard. Both will have the same width (★). One piece will have a slit; the other will not have a slit but will be the same length as the slit (we will provide specific dimensions per project).

2 Place the two pieces of cardboard together and wind the yarn around them (the first rotation starts from the top).

3 When you complete winding, secure the end of the yarn.

4 Remove the cardboard without the slit, and tie the center of the wound yarn with heavy-duty thread.

5 Remove the cardboard with the slit and snip the yarn along the center of each ring.

6 To hide the knot, use the felting needle on the yarn near the knot.

Forming Shapes with Glue

• Reinforcement Method

When cutting out delicate shapes from felt, it helps to add a thin layer of glue on the surface of the felt with a tool like a bamboo stick. Start with one side, let dry and repeat on the other side. This reinforces and hardens the fabric to allow for more intricate cuts.

• Forming shapes

Apply glue to felt and form into shapes like ears and feet before the glue dries. Secure with clips while the pieces dry.

Pom Pom Techniques ③

Attachment Methods

To attach ears, snout/muzzle, and heads to bodies.

A

1 Take the end of the pom pom string and thread a yarn needle. Insert the needle into the center of the other pom pom, through the string loop and pull tight.

2 Tightly tie the other end of the string from the first pom pom and form a knot.

B

1 Take both ends of the string from a pom pom and thread a yarn needle (alternatively, use a crochet hook). Insert needle into the connecting pom pom through the center string loop.

2 Pull the strings from the first pom pom, apply glue between the two pom poms, then continue to pull the strings tightly. Separate the yarn at the base a little.

3 Tie the strings twice.

Final steps for both A, B

1 Once tied, clip the strings as close to the knot as possible and lightly apply glue.

2 Hide the knot by rearranging the yarn.

Connecting position for snout/muzzle

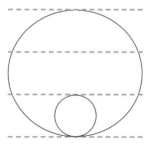

Attach the snout/muzzle around the lower ⅓ of the face.

How to Use a Felting Needle

The texture created with a felting needle on yarn and wool roving is handy for a variety of techniques.

Create legs and noses with pipe cleaners

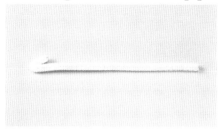

1 Bend one end of a pipe cleaner.

2 Wrap the entire pipe cleaner with wool roving.

3 Place on top of a felting mat (or a sponge if you don't have a mat), and stab with the needle. Repeat steps 2 and 3 to make sure the pipe cleaner doesn't poke out from the tips.

Using the needle on Pom Poms, forming shapes, hardening

To create indentations or for a hardened finish, use the needle to lightly stab the area. Trim the surface to even it out.

Felted snout/muzzle

Lightly felt towards the center of the snout/muzzle. Trim the surface to even it out.

Place between cardboard and felt

Place thin or small parts between two pieces of cardboard and stab with the needle to avoid unwanted finger stabbings. When felting thin shapes, try bending the edge of the cardboard a little to make felting a little easier.

> **Point**
> • To felt yarn→use short, light stabs and check often to make sure you haven't felted too much. Felting is irreversible.
> • To felt wool roving→firm stabbing is OK. If you think you've overdone the felting, simply add more roving or trim off the surface.

Felted noses and legs

1 Separate the yarn, insert the felted piece and using the felting needle, stab the base of the piece into the pom pom.
2 Arrange and lightly stab the surrounding yarn around the felted piece and blend in.

Many Expressions Depend on Eye Placement

The position of the eyes can make all the difference in the world when it comes to expression. Set them wider apart or closer together to see how varied the looks can be. Use pins to temporarily mark the eye placement and find your favorite expressions!

Little eyes

Big eyes

The position of the eyes could differ based on the species as well. For example, carnivores like lions have eyes facing frontward, while rabbits/rodents and other herbivores tend to have eyes on the sides.

Same placement, different sizes

Temporarily mark eyes, nose, ears first

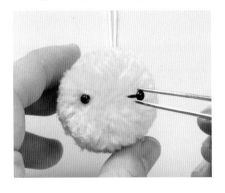

1 Use pins or a marking tool to determine position.
2 Insert part into the marked position without gluing (trimming the pom pom with the parts inserted makes it easier to create the desired expression).
3 Glue in place
※ If you want to change the placement, make sure to rearrange and smooth out the yarn with tweezers before re-inserting.

How to Use These Instructions

Completed Project Reference Page

Templates, Winding Diagram Page

Materials List

Please see p. 39 for yarn details. Color names and numbers are included within parentheses ( ).

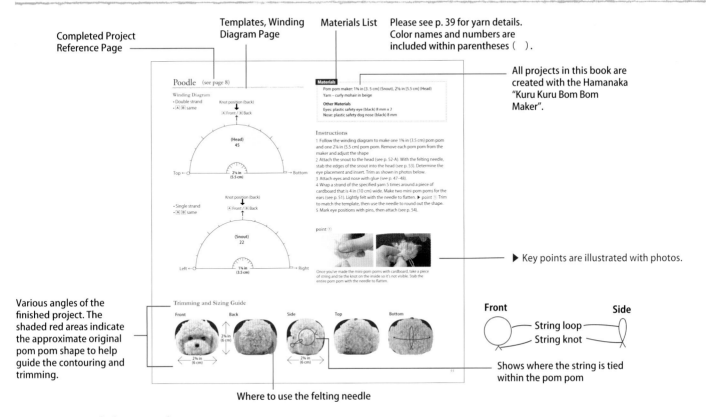

All projects in this book are created with the Hamanaka "Kuru Kuru Bom Bom Maker".

▶ Key points are illustrated with photos.

Various angles of the finished project. The shaded red areas indicate the approximate original pom pom shape to help guide the contouring and trimming.

Where to use the felting needle

Front   **Side**

String loop
String knot

Shows where the string is tied within the pom pom

How to Read the Winding Diagrams

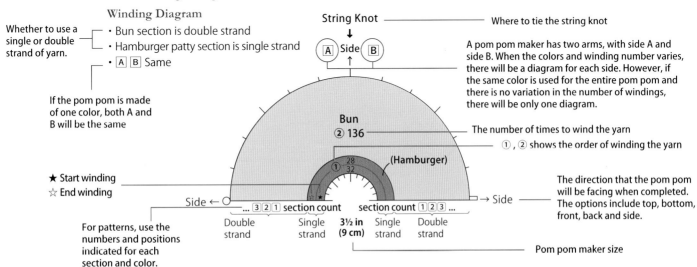

Whether to use a single or double strand of yarn.
- Bun section is double strand
- Hamburger patty section is single strand
- A B Same

If the pom pom is made of one color, both A and B will be the same

★ Start winding
☆ End winding

For patterns, use the numbers and positions indicated for each section and color.

String Knot — Where to tie the string knot

A pom pom maker has two arms, with side A and side B. When the colors and winding number varies, there will be a diagram for each side. However, if the same color is used for the entire pom pom and there is no variation in the number of windings, there will be only one diagram.

The number of times to wind the yarn

①, ② shows the order of winding the yarn

The direction that the pom pom will be facing when completed. The options include top, bottom, front, back and side.

Pom pom maker size

Sheep (see page 7)

(Template on page 93)

Winding Diagram

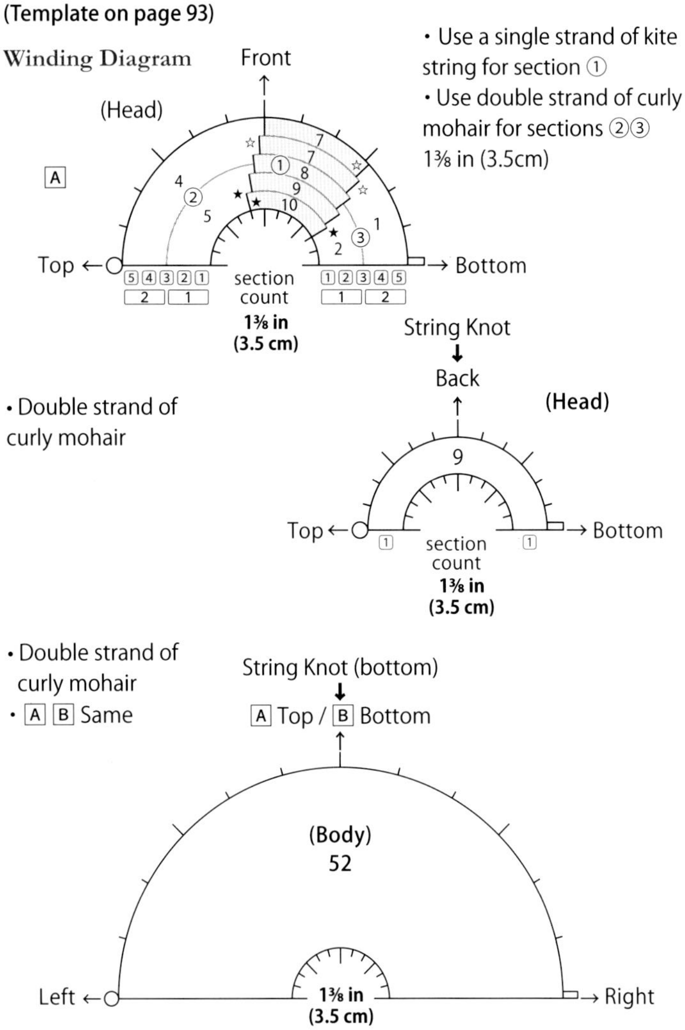

(Head)

A

- Use a single strand of kite string for section ①
- Use double strand of curly mohair for sections ②③ 1⅜ in (3.5cm)

Front

Top ← ⑤④③②① section count ①②③④⑤ → Bottom
2 | 1   1 | 2
1⅜ in (3.5 cm)

String Knot
↓
Back
↑
(Head)

- Double strand of curly mohair

9

Top ← ① section count ① → Bottom
1⅜ in (3.5 cm)

- Double strand of curly mohair
- A B Same

String Knot (bottom)
↓
A Top / B Bottom

(Body)
52

Left ← ○ 1⅜ in (3.5 cm) → Right

Trimming and Sizing Guide

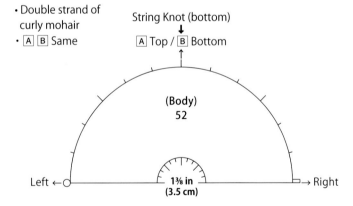

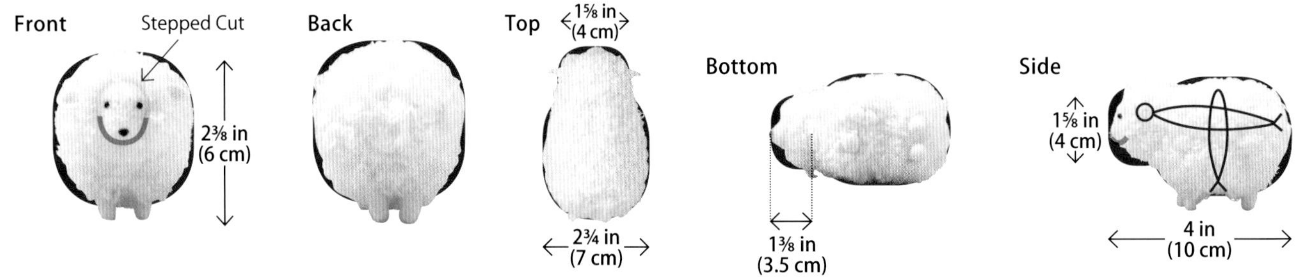

Front   Stepped Cut   Back   Top   1⅝ in (4 cm)

2⅜ in (6 cm)

2¾ in (7 cm)

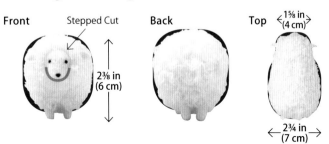

Bottom   Side

1⅜ in (3.5 cm)

1⅝ in (4 cm)

4 in (10 cm)

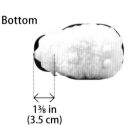

Materials

Pom pom maker: 1⅜ in [3.5 cm] (head), 2⅛ in [5.5 cm] (body)
Yarn – Head, Body: curly mohair in white
         Face: pom pom yarn in white

Other Materials
Eyes: plastic safety eye (black) 3 mm x 2
Nose: plastic safety nose (brown) 4 mm
Ears: felt (white) 2 x 1⅝ in (5 x 4 cm)
※Optional: add a touch of pink to the inside of the ears with a colored pencil

Instructions

1 Follow the winding diagram and make one 1⅜ in (3.5 cm) pom pom for the head and another 2⅛ in (5.5 cm) pom pom for the body. Remove from the pom pom makers and adjust the shape a little.
2 Attach the head to the body (see p. 52-A).
3 Lightly felt the body with a felting needle. Trim any loose yarn.
4 Shape the face using the stepped cut (see p. 50).
5 Determine the positions for the eyes and nose and attach with glue (see p. 47–48).
6 Take a small ball of wool roving, place between two pieces of cardboard and using the template, felt into legs. Create 4 legs. ▶ point ① For the ears, use the template to cut them out of felt, then add a dab of glue at the bottom section of the ears, clip and let dry (see p. 74 – point ③). Use pins to mark ear positions (see p. 49) and attach the ears with glue.
7 Glue the legs from step 6 to the body. ▶ point ②

point ①

point ②

By placing them between cardboard, felting small pieces is made easier.

Position the legs so that the sheep can stand upright. Attach legs with glue.

Poodle (see page 8)

Winding Diagram

- Double strand
- A B same

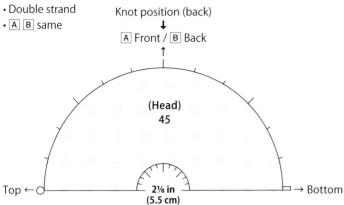

Knot position (back) ↓

A Front / B Back

(Head)
45

Top ←○   2⅛ in (5.5 cm)   □→ Bottom

- Single strand
- A B same

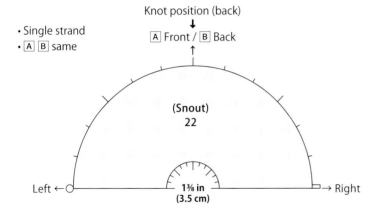

Knot position (back) ↓

A Front / B Back

(Snout)
22

Left ←○   1⅜ in (3.5 cm)   □→ Right

Materials

Pom pom maker: 1⅜ in [3.5 cm] (Snout), 2⅛ in [5.5 cm] (Head)
Yarn – curly mohair in beige

Other Materials
Eyes: plastic safety eye (black) 8 mm x 2
Nose: plastic safety dog nose (black) 8 mm

Instructions

1 Follow the winding diagram to make one 1⅜ in (3.5 cm) pom pom and one 2⅛ in (5.5 cm) pom pom. Remove each pom pom from the maker and adjust the shape

2 Attach the snout to the head (see p. 52-A). With the felting needle, stab the edges of the snout into the head (see p. 53). Determine the eye placement and insert. Trim as shown in photos below.

3 Attach eyes and nose with glue (see p. 47–48).

4 Wrap a strand of the specified yarn 5 times around a piece of cardboard that is 4 in (10 cm) wide. Make two mini-pom poms for the ears (see p. 51). Lightly felt with the needle to flatten. ▶ point ① Trim to match the template, then use the needle to round out the shape.

5 Mark eye positions with pins, then attach (see p. 54).

point ①

Once you've made the mini-pom poms with cardboard, take a piece of string and tie the knot on the inside so it's not visible. Stab the entire pom pom with the needle to flatten.

Trimming and Sizing Guide

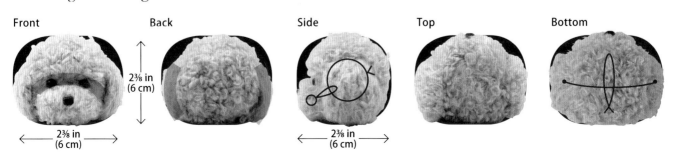

Front   Back   Side   Top   Bottom

2⅜ in (6 cm)

2⅜ in (6 cm)

2⅜ in (6 cm)

Miniature Schnauzer (see page 9)

(Template on page 94   Winding Diagram on page 92)

Materials

Pom pom maker: 2⅛ in [5.5 cm] (Snout, head)
Yarn – Ears and head: machine washable merino in light gray
    Snout: pom pom yarn in white

Other Materials
Eyes: plastic safety eye (black) 8 mm x 2
Nose: plastic safety dog nose (black) 10 mm
Ears: wool roving in gray - small amount

Instructions

1 Follow the winding diagram to make two 2⅛ in (5.5 cm) pom poms. Remove from pom pom maker and adjust shape.

2 Attach snout to head (see p. 52-A). Stab the edges of the snout into the head with the felting needle (see p. 53).

3 Use the stepped cut method to create the eyebrows (see p. 50). Trim as shown in the photos below.

4 Wrap a strand of the specified yarn 20 times around a piece of cardboard that is 3⅛ in (8 cm) wide. Make two mini-pom poms for the ears. Layer thin pieces of wool roving and lightly felt with the needle. Wrap in a separate piece of cardboard and felt some more. ▶ point ①

5 Use the template and cut out the ears. Fold each ear along line indicated on template. Felt the folded section, stabbing from above. Temporarily mark ear positions with pins. Thread the loose ends of the ear pom pom string into a yarn needle and attach to the head using the marking pins as a guide.

6 Determine the eyes and nose placements and attach with glue (see p. 47–48).

point ①

1

Clip two strands of heavy duty thread across the top of a piece of cardboard. Wrap the specified yarn (for the ears in this case) around the cardboard. When done, tie the threads tightly at the top.

2

Adjust the yarn, layer a thin piece of wool roving on top and flatten by felting with the needle (the felted portion will be the underside of the ear).

3

Place ear between another piece of cardboard and felt some more.

Trimming and Sizing Guide

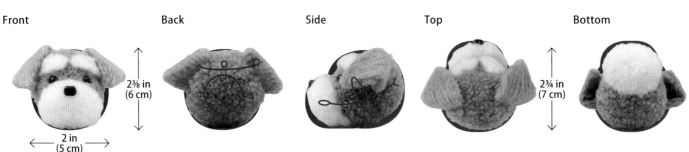

Front

2 in
(5 cm)

2⅜ in
(6 cm)

Back

Side

Top

Bottom

2¾ in
(7 cm)

Bear (see page 12)

Winding Diagram
- Double strand
- A B same

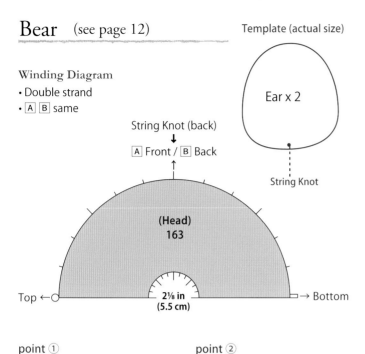

Template (actual size)

Ear x 2

String Knot (back)
↓
A Front / B Back

String Knot

(Head)
163

Top ←○

2⅛ in
(5.5 cm)

→ Bottom

Materials
Pom pom maker: 2⅛ in (5.5 cm)
Yarn – pom pom yarn in beige

Other Materials
Eyes: plastic safety eye (black) 6 mm x 2
Nose: plastic safety nose (brown) 9 mm

Instructions

1 Follow winding diagram and make a 2⅛ in (5.5 cm) pom pom. Remove from pom pom maker, adjust shape and trim as shown in photos below.

2 Wrap a single strand of the specified yarn 28 times around a 1⅜ in (3.5 cm)-wide cardboard piece. This is the snout pom pom.

3 Attach the snout to the head (see p. 52-A). Felt the snout.

4 Wrap a single strand of the specified yarn 22 times around a 1⅜ in (3.5 cm)-wide cardboard piece. Make two pom poms for the ears. Place between cardboard and felt, flattening the ear pieces.

5 Determine the eye placement and attach with glue (see p. 47–48). Use pins to temporarily mark ear placement. ▶ point ①

6 Thread the string from the ear pom pom into a yarn needle and attach to the head (see p. 72 point ①). ▶ point ②

7 Trim the surface with the finish cut method (see p. 50), determine the nose position and attach with glue.

point ①

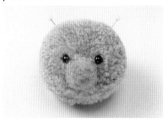

Place the ears more towards the top of the head. You can still adjust the position somewhat even after the ears are attached.

point ②

Make sure to attach the ear with the string knot underneath to hide it.

Trimming and Sizing Guide

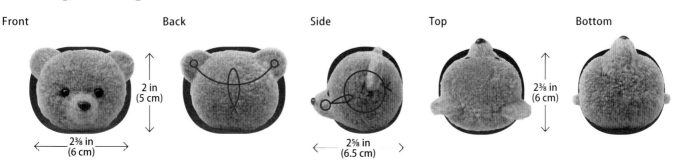

Front

Back

2 in
(5 cm)

Side

Top

2⅜ in
(6 cm)

Bottom

2⅜ in
(6 cm)

2⅝ in
(6.5 cm)

Calico Cat (see page 10)

(Template on page 94   Winding Diagram on page 90)

Materials

Pom pom maker 2⅛ in (5.5 cm)
Yarn – pom pom yarn in white, beige and black

Other Materials

Eyes: crystal eyes in gold in 9 mm x 2
Ears: felt (black) 7 x 4⅜ in (18 x 11 cm), (camel) 3⅛ x 4⅜ in (8 x 11 cm)
Nose, mouth: wool roving (a: light pink, b: apricot/peach
c: brown) - a small amount each

Trimming and Sizing Guide

Front

Back

2⅛ in
(5.5 cm)

← 2⅜ in →
(6 cm)

Side

← 2⅜ in →
(6 cm)

Top

Bottom

2 in
(5 cm)

Brown Tiger Cat   (see page 11)

(Template on page 94   Winding Diagram on page 91)

Materials

Pom pom maker 2⅛ in (5.5 cm)
Yarn – pom pom yarn in light beige and white
        alpaca merino in camel

Other Materials

Eyes: cat's eyes in blue 9 mm x 2
Ears: felt (camel) 6¼ x 8⅝ in (16 x 22 cm)
Nose, mouth: wool roving (a: light pink, b: apricot/peach
c: brown d: biscuit) - a small amount each

Trimming and Sizing Guide

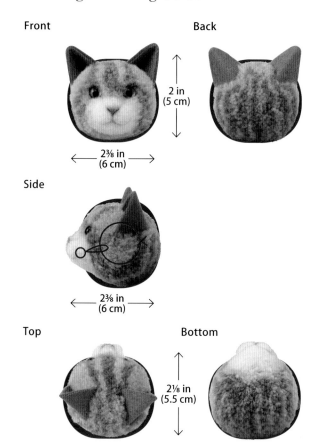

Front

Back

2 in
(5 cm)

← 2⅜ in →
(6 cm)

Side

← 2⅜ in →
(6 cm)

Top

Bottom

2⅛ in
(5.5 cm)

Instructions

1 Follow the winding diagram and make a 2⅛ in (5.5 cm) pom pom. Remove from pom pom maker and adjust the shape.

2 Wind the white yarn 40 times around a 1⅜ in (3.5 cm)-wide cardboard piece for the snout pom pom.

3 Attach snout to head (see p. 52-A). ▶ **point** ①

4 Felt the muzzle with a felting needle and trim as shown in photos on p. 60. ▶ **point** ② Temporarily determine eye placement and insert eye pieces.

5 Determine nose placement. Take a very small amount of wool roving a and felt into an upside-down triangle onto the snout. Trim off excess. Place roving b on top of triangle and felt. Again, trim off excess. ▶ **steps 1 and 2 from point** ③

6 Felt a very small amount of roving c beneath the nose and shape the line beneath the nose. Felt with roving d to form the curve of the mouth (use roving c for the calico cat). Adjust the eyes, nose area and snout to your liking with needle.

7 Cut out the ears using the template. Glue two pieces together for each ear, bend and let dry.

8 Determine ear placement, separate the yarn of that section (see p. 49) and attach with glue. Glue the eyes in at this point as well. Using the felting needle, lightly stab an outline above the eyes, creating "eyelids" (for the calico cat, felt roving c above and at the corner of the eyes). ▶ **point** ④ Lightly felt beneath the nose as well.

point ①

Tie the string under the chin when attaching the snout to the head. Tie the knot as tightly as possible.

point ②

From left to right: the snout initially attached to head; trimming of the nose and mouth area in progress; completed. Stop and check frequently as you trim the nose, mouth and head areas.

point ③

1

Felt the light pink wool roving into an upside down triangular shape. Trim excess.

2

Place apricot roving on top of triangle and continue felting. Trim excess.

3

Curve the brown wool roving (for the Brown Tiger Cat, use biscuit-colored roving) into a mouth.

point ④

Press the section above the eye with your finger in a way that allows the yarn to tuft up and use the needle to lightly felt an outline around the eyes.

Lion (see page 13)

(Template on page 94)

Winding Diagram

- Double strand
- A B same

String Knot (bottom)
↓
A Top / B Bottom

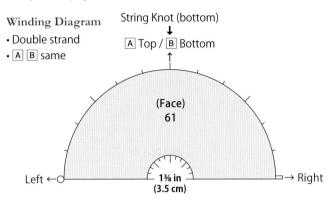

(Face)
61

Left ← ○   ○ → Right

1⅜ in
(3.5 cm)

- Double strand
- A B same

String Knot (bottom)
↓
A Top / B Bottom

※See p. 43–2 for yarn winding instructions

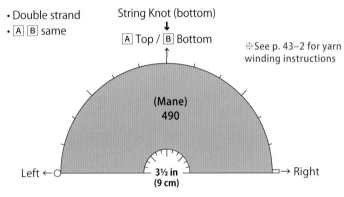

(Mane)
490

Left ← ○   ○ → Right

3½ in
(9 cm)

Trimming and Sizing Guide

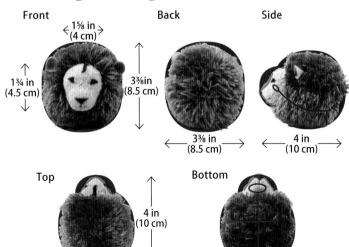

Front
← 1⅝ in →
(4 cm)

↑
1¾ in
(4.5 cm)
↓

Back

↑
3⅜ in
(8.5 cm)
↓

← 3⅜ in →
(8.5 cm)

Side

← 4 in →
(10 cm)

Top

Bottom

↑
4 in
(10 cm)
↓

Materials

Pom pom maker 1⅜ in (3.5 cm) (face), 3½ in (9 cm) (mane)
Yarn — Face: pom pom yarn in light beige
   Mane: mohair in brown →2 balls/ skeins
   Detail between eyes: pom pom yarn in brown, 1 in (2.5 cm)
   x 8 strands

Other Materials
Eyes: plastic safety eye (black) 3 mm x 2; felt (dark brown)
⅜ x 1 in (1 x 2.5 cm)
Nose: felt (black) ⅜ x ⅞ in (1 x 2 cm)
Ears: felt (tan) 2⅜ x 2¾ in (6 x 7 cm)
Mouth: heavy duty thread (black) 12⅝ in (32 cm)

Instructions

1 Follow winding diagram and make one 1⅜ in (3.5 cm) pom pom and one 3½ in (9 cm) pom pom. Remove from pom pom maker and adjust shape.

2 With the blue line shown in the lower left photos as a guide, use a felting needle to shape the face. Trim (see p. 53- ①).

3 Add the detail between the eyes. ▶ point ① Apply glue on both sides of the black felt. Once dry, cut out eyes and nose using the templates. Apply another dab of glue to the base of each ear, clip each ear to pinch the bottom and let dry (see p. 74-point ③).

4 Trim the top of the head to align with the angle of the mane and attach mane to face (see p. 52-B).

5 Punch a hole in the felt pieces for the eyes with an awl or similar tool. Insert and glue in the plastic safety eye in each felt piece. Determine the eye and nose placement and attach with glue (see p. 48).

6 Create the mouth with the heavy duty thread. Clip the thread ends close to the knot and apply a dab of glue. ▶ point ② Determine the ear placement and attach the dried pieces from step 3 with glue (see p. 49).

7 Gently thin the mane with scissors and adjust the shape.

point ①

Separate the yarn and felt the brown thread at the base one strand at a time with the needle. Repeat with all 8 strands and trim excess.

point ②

Loop the thread once and repeat. Then create a line from the mouth to the nose with a felting needle.

Monkey (page 14)

Template (actual size)
Nose

Winding Diagram

· Single strand for the light beige of section ①
· Double strand for the light brown of section ②~⑤

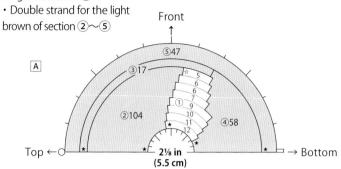

A

Front ↑

⑤47
③17
☆ 5
6
6
7
① 8
9
10
★ 11
12
②104
④58

Top ←O   2⅛ in (5.5 cm)   → Bottom

· Double strand of light brown yarn

String Knot (bottom)
↓
Bottom ↑

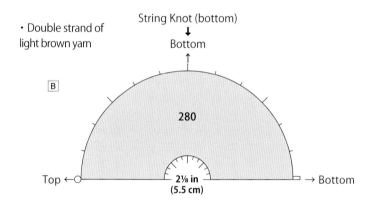

B

280

Top ←O   2⅛ in (5.5 cm)   → Bottom

Materials

Pom pom maker: 2⅛ in (5.5 cm)
Yarn – Head: hairy/fuzzy alpaca fingering wool in light brown
Face, snout: pom pom yarn in light beige

Other Materials
Eyes: plastic safety eye (black) 6 mm x 2
Nose: felt (black) ⅜ x ⅞ in (1 x 2 cm)
Mouth: heavy duty thread (black) as needed

Instructions

1 Follow winding diagram and make one 2⅛ in (5.5 cm) pom pom. Remove from pom pom maker and adjust shape.
2 Wrap specified yarn 30 times around a 1⅛ in (3 cm)-wide cardboard piece to make the snout pom pom (see p. 51). Attach snout to face (see p. 52).
3 Trim the border between the head and face using the stepped cut method (see p. 50).
4 Use a felting needle on the snout to shape it as shown in the photos below (see p. 53).
5 Determine the eye placement and temporarily insert the plastic eye pieces (see p. 47). Shape the face by trimming and using the felting needle. Felt to outline the eyes and form the line under the nose.
▶ point ① See point ② section for the Lion to create the mouth (p. 62).
6 Attach the eyes with glue. Also attach the glue-reinforced nose (see p. 51).

Trimming and Sizing Guide

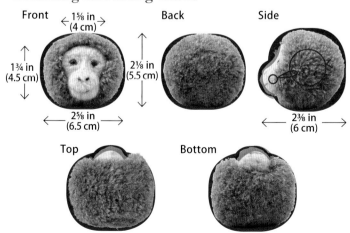

Front
← 1⅝ in (4 cm) →
1¾ in (4.5 cm)
← 2⅝ in (6.5 cm) →

Back
2⅛ in (5.5 cm)

Side
← 2⅜ in (6 cm) →

Top

Bottom

point ①

1

Insert eyes and trim the surrounding area a little.
※ Tuft up the corners of the eyes a little.

2

Pinch some yarn with tweezers to create the line under the nose, then felt with a needle.

3

Outline the eyes with a felting needle.

Elephant (see page 15)

(Template on page 94)

Trimming and Sizing Guide

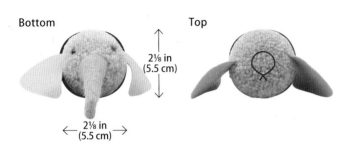

Bottom

Top

2⅛ in
(5.5 cm)

2⅛ in
(5.5 cm)

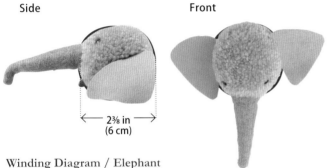

Side

Front

2⅜ in
(6 cm)

Winding Diagram / Elephant

- Double strand
- A B same

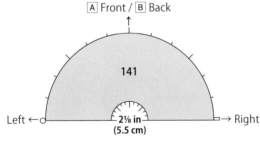

String Knot (Back)
↓
A Front / B Back

141

Left ←○ 2⅛ in ○→ Right
(5.5 cm)

Materials

Pom pom maker: 2⅛ in (5.5 cm)
Yarn – machine washable merino worsted weight in light gray

Other Materials
Eyes: plastic safety eye (black) 6 mm x 2
Ears: felt (gray) 3⅛ x 5½ in (8 x 14 cm)
Nose: wool roving (light gray)
Pipe cleaner 3⅛ in (8 cm)

Instructions

1 Follow winding diagram and make one 2⅛ in (5.5 cm) pom pom. Remove from pom pom maker and adjust shape. Trim as shown in left photo.

2 Wrap pipe cleaner with wool roving and using the template, felt with the needle to make the nose (see p. 53). Cut out the ears using the template.

3 Attach nose to head with the felting needle. ▶ point ①

4 Determine the eye placement and attach with glue (see p. 47–48)

5 Mark ear placement with pins (see p. 49), then attach ears with glue.

point ①

1

2

Determine nose position and separate out the yarn at the base.

Felt the nose into place with the felting needle. Rearrange the surrounding yarn and blend in with the needle.

Winding Diagram / Cat

- Double strand
- A B same

- Double strand
- A B same

※ See p. 43-2 for yarn winding instructions

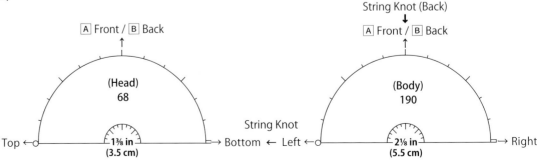

A Front / B Back

(Head)
68

Top ←○ 1⅜ in →⊢ Bottom
(3.5 cm)

String Knot (Back)
↓
A Front / B Back

(Body)
190

String Knot

Left ←○ 2⅛ in ○→ Right
(5.5 cm)

Cat (see page 16)

(Template on page 94   Winding Diagram on page 64)

Materials

Pom pom maker: Head: 1⅜ in (3.5 cm), Body: 2⅛ in (5.5 cm)
Yarn – pom pom yarn in white, 1 ball/skein

Other Materials
Eyes: cat's eye (gold) 7.5 mm x 2
Nose: wool roving (light pink, apricot)
Mouth: wool roving (brown)
Ears: felt (white) 1⅛ x 3 in (3 x 7 cm)
※ add a touch of color inside the ear with a pink colored pencil
Legs, tail: wool roving (white 66WH)
Pipe cleaner (for tail) 4 in (10 cm)

Instructions

1 Follow winding diagram instructions and make one 1⅜ in (3.5 cm) pom pom and one 2⅛ in (5.5 cm) pom pom. Remove from pom pom maker and adjust shape.

2 Wrap a single strand of specified yarn 26 times around a 1 in (2.5 cm)-wide cardboard piece to make the snout mini-pom pom (see p 51). Attach snout to head (see p. 52).

3 Refer to instructions from the Calico Cat/Brown Tiger Cat (p. 60–61) to trim and felt the face.

4 Cut out ears using template and add some pink with a colored pencil. Apply a dab of glue at the base of the ear, fold and let dry.

5 Roughly trim the body as shown in the photos at right and below.
▶ point ①   Attach ears to the head with glue.

6 Attach head to body (see p. 52-B).

7 Use the felting needle around the neckline (see p. 53). Trim and refer to the left photo for the overall shape.

8 Create legs and tail out of wool roving. ▶ point ② Use the felting needle to attach the front two legs to the body. ▶ point ③ Attach back legs and tail with glue.

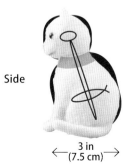

Side

3 in
(7.5 cm)

point ①

Trim the section where the legs will be attached into a "V" shape. Trim the body to give an overall rounded appearance.

point ②

Wrap wool roving around a pipe cleaner and felt to make the tail (see p. 53). Take a piece of wool roving to match the template and felt to make legs.

point ③

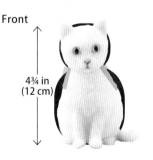

Shape the front legs to fit at a nice angle around the chest area and attach with the felting needle. Separate the yarn and use the needle to stab the base of the legs into the body from below.

Trimming and Sizing Guide

Front

4¾ in
(12 cm)

Back

1⅝ in
(4 cm)

1⅝ in
(4 cm)

2⅜ in
(6 cm)

Top

1¾ in
(4.5 cm)

Bottom

Dachshund (see page 17)

(Template on page 94)

Winding Diagram

- Double strand
- A B same

String Knot (Bottom)
↓
A Top / B Bottom
↑

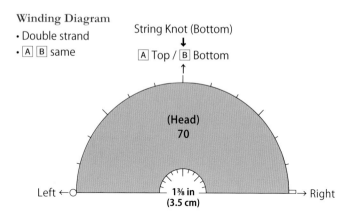

(Head)
70

Left ←○   1⅜ in   ○→ Right
                 (3.5 cm)

- Double strand
- A B same

String Knot (Bottom)
↓
A Top / B Bottom

※See p. 43-2 for yarn winding instructions

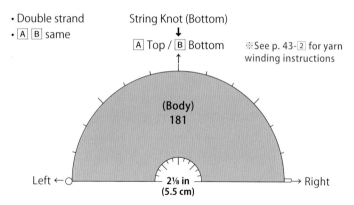

(Body)
181

Left ←○   2⅛ in   ○→ Right
                 (5.5 cm)

Materials

Pom pom maker: Head: 1⅜ in (3.5 cm), Body: 2⅛ in (5.5 cm)
Yarn – pom pom yarn in beige, 2 balls/skeins

Other Materials
Eyes: plastic safety eye (black) 8 mm x 2
Nose: plastic safety dog nose (black) 8 mm
Legs, tail: wool roving (light tan/biscuit)

Instructions

1 Follow winding diagram and make one 1⅜ in (3.5 cm) pom pom and one 2⅛ in (5.5 cm) pom pom. Remove from pom pom maker and adjust shape. Wrap a single strand of specified yarn 5 times around a 4 in (10 cm)-wide piece of cardboard. Tie the top off with heavy duty thread and felt with a needle (see p. 51). Cut using template. ▶ **point ①**

2 Felt as shown in photo, and trim to form snout. ▶ **point ②**
Determine eye placement and temporarily insert eye pieces. Trim and felt the head. Mark ear placement with pins and attach ears to head with yarn needle and thread from ear pom poms (see p. 72-point ①). Add a dab of glue at the inner base of the ears to secure.

3 Attach eyes and nose with glue. Roughly trim the body as shown in photo below. Attach head to body (see p. 52-B). Trim and felt as shown in photo to shape body.

4 Use the template to felt the wool roving into the legs and tail.

5 Attach front legs to body with the felting needle (see p. 53). Attach back legs and tail with glue.

point ①   point ②

Arrange the knot underneath and evenly felt the entire ear.

Firmly felt the nose area, then trim with scissors.

Trimming and Sizing Guide

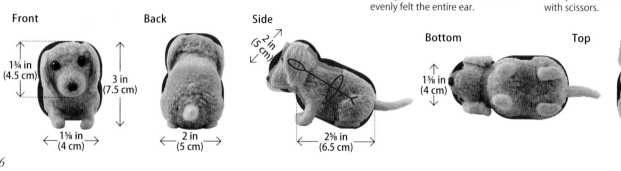

Front

1¾ in (4.5 cm)

3 in (7.5 cm)

1⅝ in (4 cm)

Back

2 in (5 cm)

Side

2 in (5 cm)

2⅝ in (6.5 cm)

Bottom

1⅝ in (4 cm)

Top

2⅜ in (6 cm)

Penguin (see page 18)

(Template on page 95   Winding Diagram on page 91)

Materials

Pom pom maker: Head: 1⅜ in (3.5 cm), Body: 2⅛ in (5.5 cm)
Yarn – pom pom yarn in black. white and pale brown

Other Materials
Eyes: plastic safety eye (black) 4 mm x 2
Wing: felt (gray) 2⅜ x 2¾ in (6 x 7 cm)
Beak, feet: felt (black) 2⅜ x 2¾ in (6 x 7 cm)

Instructions

1 Follow winding diagram and make one 1⅜ (3.5 cm) pom pom and one 2⅛ in (5.5 cm). Remove from pom pom maker and adjust shape.
2 Attach head to body. ▶ point ①
3 Trim as shown in right photo.
4 Determine eye placement and temporarily insert plastic safety eyes (see p. 47).
5 Cut out beak, wings and feet using templates. Reinforce beak with glue (see p. 51), give it some shape and let dry. Attach the parts to the body with glue.
6 Attach eyes with glue (see p. 48).

point ①

Connect the head to the body using a crochet hook and the string from the head. Add glue to secure the connection.

Tie twice, cut the string short and add a dab of glue to the knot.

Trimming and Sizing Guide

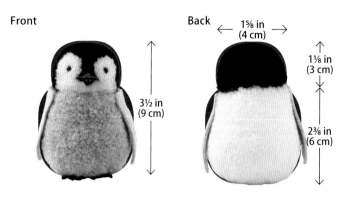

Front

Back   ← 1⅝ in (4 cm) →

1⅛ in (3 cm)

3½ in (9 cm)

2⅜ in (6 cm)

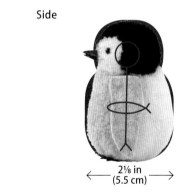

Side

2⅛ in (5.5 cm)

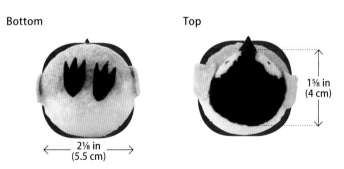

Bottom

Top

1⅝ in (4 cm)

2⅛ in (5.5 cm)

67

Seal (see page 19)

(Template on page 95)

Winding Diagram
(Head)

- Double strand for off-white in sections ①②③⑤⑥
- Single strand for black in section ④

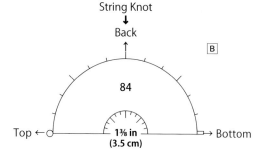

Front

44

14

7 | 14 | ⑤ | 7
15 | ①

A

Top ← ⑦ ⑤ ③ ① ★ 1⅜ in ② ① ③ ⑤ ⑦ → Bottom
6 3 1 (3.5 cm) 2 1 3 5 7

String Knot
↓
Back

B

84

Top ← 1⅜ in → Bottom
(3.5 cm)

- Double strand
- A B same

String Knot (Bottom)
↓
A Top / B Bottom

※See p. 43-2 for yarn winding instructions

(Body)
310

Left ← 2¾ in → Right
(7 cm)

Materials

Pom pom maker: Head: 1⅜ in (3.5 cm), Body: 2¾ in (7 cm)
Yarn – machine washable sport weight in off-weight 2 balls/skeins
machine washable sport weight in black

Other Materials
Eyes: plastic safety eye (black) 6 mm x 2
Nose: plastic safety nose (black) 6 mm
Front legs, tail fin: felt (off-white) 2¾ x 3½ in (7 x 9 cm)

Instructions

1 Follow winding diagram and make one 1⅜ in (3.5 cm) and one 2¾ in (7 cm) pom pom. Wrap a single strand of the specified yarn 34 times around a 1 in (2.5 cm)-wide cardboard piece and make a mini-pom pom for the snout (see p. 51).

2 Attach snout to head (see p. 52-A). Felt the muzzle (see p. 53). Trim as shown in photos below. Attach eyes and nose with glue (see p. 47–48).

3 Attach head to body. ▶ point ① Roughly trim the body. Felt the back and tail fin areas and trim as shown in photos below.

4 Cut out front legs and tail fin using templates and attach with glue.

point ①

Keep the tail string from the head pom pom after connecting the snout. Use this string to then attach the head to the body. Once they are connected, cut the string from the body pom pom.

Trimming and Sizing Guide

Front | Back | Side | Top | Bottom

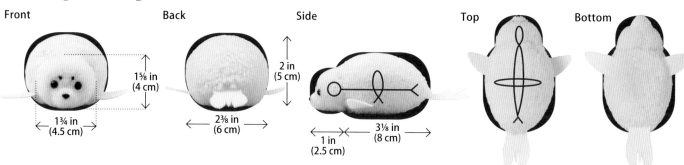

Front: 1⅝ in (4 cm), 1¾ in (4.5 cm)

Back: 2⅜ in (6 cm), 2 in (5 cm)

Side: 3⅛ in (8 cm), 1 in (2.5 cm)

Tropical Fish (see page 20)

(Template on page 95)

Winding Diagram

- White for section ①,
  black for section ②
- Double strand

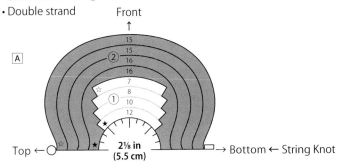

Ⓐ

Front ↑

15
② 15
16
16
7
① 8
10
12

Top ← ○   ★   2⅛ in
(5.5 cm)   → Bottom ← String Knot

- White for sections ① ③,
  black for section ②
- Double strand

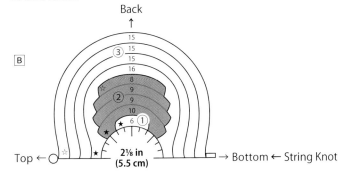

Ⓑ

Back ↑

15
③ 15
15
16
8
② 9
9
10
★ 6 ①

Top ← ○   ★   2⅛ in
(5.5 cm)   → Bottom ← String Knot

Materials

Pom pom maker: 2⅛ in (5.5 cm)
Yarn – Machine washable merino worsted weight in white and black

Other Materials
Eyes: plastic eye (brown) 4.5 mm x 2
Dorsal fin ①: felt (white) 2¾ x 4⅜ in (7 x 11 cm)
Chest fin, dorsal fin ②, tail fin: felt (yellow) 1⅝ x 3⅛ in (4 x 8 cm)
Stomach fin, lower fin: felt (black) 1⅛ x 2¾ in (3 x 7 cm)

Instructions

1 Follow winding diagram and make a 2⅛ in (5.5 cm) pom pom. ▶
point ① Remove from pom pom maker and adjust shape (see p. 50).
2 While keeping an eye on the direction of the string, trim as shown in the photos below.
3 For dorsal fin ①, glue two pieces of felt together and use template to cut out shape. Cut out other fins as well.
4 Using the photo below as a guide, attach the fins with glue.
5 Attach eyes with glue (see p. 44).

point ①

Pay attention to the winding diagram to create the pretty pattern.

Trimming and Sizing Guide

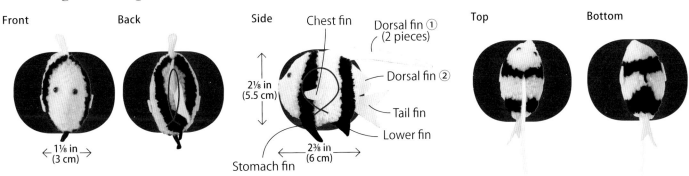

Front

Back

Side   Chest fin

Dorsal fin ①
(2 pieces)

Dorsal fin ②

Tail fin

Lower fin

Stomach fin

Top   Bottom

2⅛ in
(5.5 cm)

1⅛ in
(3 cm)

2⅜ in
(6 cm)

Puffer Fish (see page 21)

(Template on page 95)

Winding Diagram

- ① Double strand (black, black)
- ② Triple strand (black, black, light gray)
- ③ Double strand (black, light gray)
- ④ Double strand (light gray, white)
- ⑤ Single strand (white)

※ use the same colors continuously without cutting

Materials

Pom pom maker: 2⅛ in (5.5 cm)
Yarn – machine washable merino worsted weight in black, light gray and white

Other Materials
Eyes: plastic eye (brown) 4.5 mm x 2
Dorsal fin, tail fin: felt (black) 1⅝ x 3⅛ in (4 x 8 cm)
Chest fin, lower fin, mouth: felt (gray) 1⅝ x 3⅛ in (4 x 8 cm)

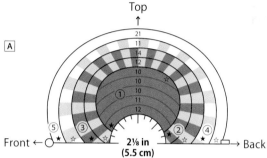

Top

A

21
11
14
12
10
10
① 10
11
12

⑤ ③ ② ④

Front ← ○ 2⅛ in (5.5 cm) → Back

- White double strand

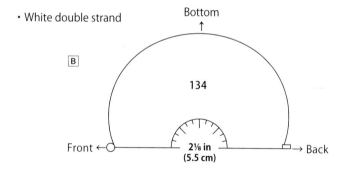

Bottom

B

134

Front ← ○ 2⅛ in (5.5 cm) → Back

Instructions

1 Follow winding diagram and make a 2⅛ in (5.5 cm) pom pom.
▶ point ① Remove from pom pom maker and adjust shape.
2 Trim into a round shape as shown in the photos below.
3 Attach the various fins with glue.
4 Attach eyes with glue (see p. 47–8).
5 Apply a thin layer or glue on both sides of the mouth felt piece, curve it a little and let dry. ▶ point ② Once dry, attach eyes with glue.

point ①

point ②

First wind two strands of black, then add a strand of light gray, then remove a strand of black, and then replace the black with a white strand. Finish off with a single strand of white.

Add curvature to the felt piece before the glue completely dries. Let the felt dry completely once the curve is formed.

Trimming and Sizing Guide

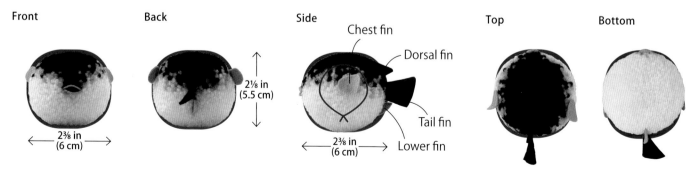

Front

Back

Side

Chest fin

Dorsal fin

Tail fin

Lower fin

2⅛ in (5.5 cm)

2⅜ in (6 cm)

2⅜ in (6 cm)

Top

Bottom

Parakeet (see page 22)

Winding Diagram

- Single strand for white in section ①
- Double strand for sky blue in sections ② ③
- Single strand for blue

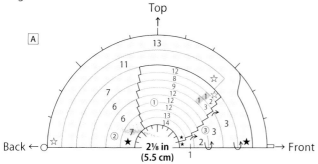

A

Top ↑

13
11
12
8
9
12
7
12
1 1 2
6
12
1 2 3
6
13
14
3
② 7
③ 3 3
Back ←○ ★ 2⅛ in ★ →2 →Front
(5.5 cm)
1

- Double strand for sky blue

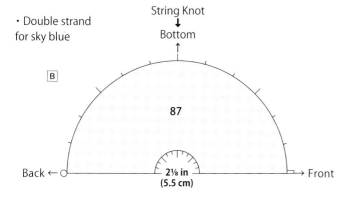

String Knot
↓
Bottom
↑

B

87

Back ←○ 2⅛ in →Front
(5.5 cm)

Materials

Pom pom maker: 2⅛ in (5.5 cm)
Yarn – machine washable merino worsted weight in white
worsted weight in blue and sky blue

Other Materials
Eyes: plastic safety eye (black) 4 mm x 2
Beak: felt (light yellow) ⅞ x ⅞ in (2 x 2 cm)

Instructions

1 Follow winding diagram and make one 2⅛ in (5.5 cm) pom pom (see p. 74-point ① on how to wind the blue yarn). Remove from pom pom maker and adjust shape. Trim as shown in photos below. ▶ point ①
2 Reinforce both sides of the felt with glue (see p. 51) and curve the felt a little and let dry.
3 Determine eye placement and attach with glue (see p. 44). Cut out beak using template. Attach a single strand of loosened sky blue yarn and attach to the upper part of the beak. Glue the beak onto the head.

point ①

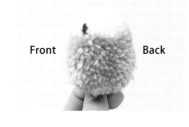

Front   Back

Trim the back so that it protrudes a bit. Shape the head to be a little smaller than the body and bulge out the bottom half.

Template (actual size)

Beak

Trimming and Sizing Guide

Front

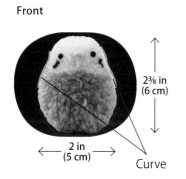

2⅜ in
(6 cm)

← 2 in →
(5 cm)
Curve

Back

← 1⅜ in →
(3.5 cm)

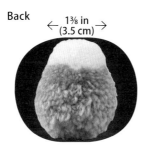

Side

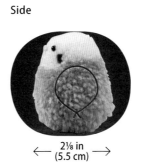

← 2⅛ in →
(5.5 cm)

Bottom

Top

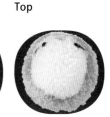

Frog (see page 23)

Winding Diagram

- Double strand for yellow-green

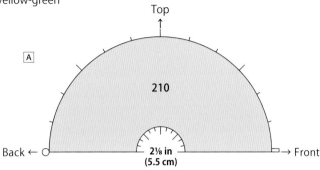

A

210

Top ↑

Back ← | → Front

2⅛ in (5.5 cm)

- Double strand for off-white

String Knot ↓ Bottom

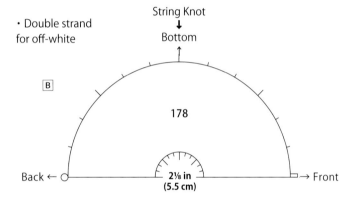

B

178

Back ← | → Front

2⅛ in (5.5 cm)

Materials

Pom pom maker: 2⅛ in (5.5 cm)
Yarn – worsted weight in yellow-green and off-white

Other Materials
Eyes: plastic eye (brown) 12 mm x 2
Nose: plastic safety nose 2 mm x 2

Instructions

1 Follow winding diagram and make a 2⅛ in (5.5 cm) pom pom.
2 Remove from pom pom maker, adjust shape and trim as shown in photos below.
3 Wrap a single strand of the specified yarn 25 times around a 1 in (2.5 cm)-wide cardboard piece and make 2 mini-pom poms for the eyes (see p. 51).
4 Mark mini-pom pom placement with pins and attach them to head. ▶ point ①
5 Trim around the eyes.
6 Determine eye position and attach with glue (see p. 47–48). Then do the same with the nose.

point ①

1

Using the photo as a guide, determine the placement of the mini-pom poms.

2

Thread the string from the mini-pom poms into a yarn needle and insert through the center string loop of the head, pulling it through to the other side.

3

Firmly tie the string ends from the mini-pom pom into a tight knot.

Trimming and Sizing Guide

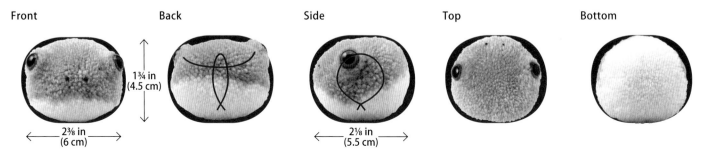

Front | Back | Side | Top | Bottom

1¾ in (4.5 cm)

2⅜ in (6 cm)

2⅛ in (5.5 cm)

Pig (see page 24)

(Template on page 95)

Winding Diagram
- Double strand
- A B Same

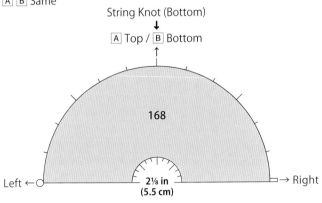

String Knot (Bottom)
↓
A Top / B Bottom
↑

168

Left ←○

2⅛ in
(5.5 cm)

→ Right

Materials
Pom pom maker: 2⅛ in (5.5 cm)
Yarn – pom pom yarn in pink

Other Materials
Eyes: plastic safety eye (black) 5 mm x 2
Nose, ears: felt (pink) 1⅜ x 2 in (3.5 x 5 cm)
Legs, tail: wool roving (light pink)

Instructions

1 Follow winding diagram and make one 2⅛ in (5.5 cm) pom pom. Remove from pom pom maker and adjust shape.
2 Felt the face using the photos below as a guide. Trim the face and body. ▶ point ①
3 Cut out nose using the template, create holes and attach with glue.
4 Determine eye placement and attach with glue (see p. 47–48).
5 Cut out ears using template. Add a dab of glue to the base of each ear, clip and let dry (see p. 74-point ③). Attach with glue (see p. 49).
6 Shape wool roving using template and make the legs and tail. Attach to the body with the felting needle.

point ①

Make one side the snout end and firmly felt using the needle. Trim the tip of the nose to flatten it to make it easier to attach the felt nose piece.

Trimming and Sizing Guide

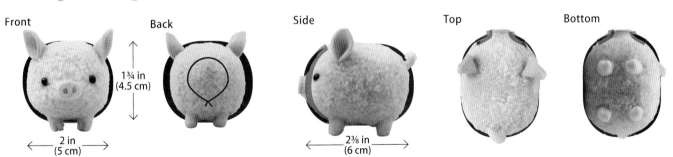

Front

Back

Side

Top

Bottom

1¾ in
(4.5 cm)

2 in
(5 cm)

2⅜ in
(6 cm)

Strawberry Bunny (see page 25)

(Template on page 95)

Winding Diagram

• Single strand for all

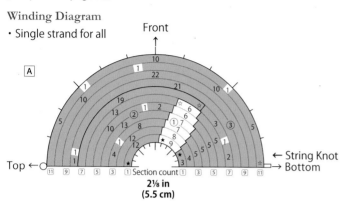

A

Front

Top ←

← String Knot
→ Bottom

2⅛ in
(5.5 cm)

• Single strand for all

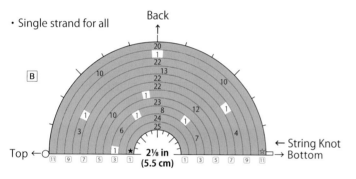

B

Back

Top ←

← String Knot
→ Bottom

2⅛ in
(5.5 cm)

Materials

Pom pom maker: 2⅛ in (5.5 cm)
Yarn – machine washable merino worsted weight in red and white

Other Materials
Eyes: safety plastic eye (black) 6 mm x 2
Nose: safety plastic eye (black) 3 mm
Ears: felt (white) 1⅝ x 2 in (4 x 5 cm)
Stem: felt (yellow green) 2¾ x 2¾ in (7 x 7 cm)

Instructions

1 Follow winding diagram and make a 2⅛ in (5.5 cm) pom pom.
▶ point ① Remove from pom pom maker and adjust shape.
2 Use the stepped cut method to make the face (see p. 50). Trim to form the strawberry shape. ▶ point ②
3 Determine the eye and nose placement and attach with glue (see p. 47–48).
4 Cut out ears from white felt using the template. Add a dab of glue at the bottom of each ear, clip the section and let dry. ▶ point ③
5 Determine the ear placement (see p. 49) and attach with glue. Cut out stem from the yellow green felt using the template and attach to the bottom with glue.

point ①

After winding a single strand of white yarn, cross it over a little and cut the yarn. Wind the red yarn on top and follow the winding diagram to intersperse the white yarn.

point ②

Mark the tip of the strawberry with a pin. Maintain that area as the highest point and roughly trim the rest of the pom pom into an approximate shape of a strawberry. Once the general shape is formed, use the finish cut method (see p. 50).

point ③

Apply the glue at the bottom section. Clip to create the ear shape while the glue hasn't set, then let fully dry.

Trimming and Sizing Guide

Front

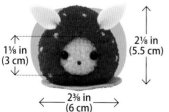

1⅛ in
(3 cm)

2⅛ in
(5.5 cm)

2⅜ in
(6 cm)

Back

Side

2⅛ in
(5.5 cm)

Top

Hamster (see page 26)

(Winding Diagram on page 92)

Materials

Pom pom maker: Head: 1⅜ in (3.5 cm), Body: 2⅛ in (5.5 cm)
Yarn – pom pom yarn in light beige and white

Other Materials
Eyes: plastic safety eye (black) 6 mm x 2
Nose: Beads (pink) ⅛ in (4 mm)
Ears: felt (beige) 1⅛ x 2⅜ in (3 x 6 cm)
Paws: felt (brown beige) 2⅜ x 1⅝ in (6 x 4 cm)

Instructions

1 Follow the winding diagram and make one 1⅜ in (3.5 cm) pom pom and one 2⅛ in (5.5 cm) pom pom. Remove from pom pom maker and adjust shape.

2 Trim the head as shown in photo on right. Roughly trim the body.

3 Attach the head to the body (see p. 52-B).

4 Trim the body as shown in photos on right. ▶ point ①

5 Determine the eyes and nose placement and attach with glue (see p. 47–48).

6 Cut out the ears using the template. Add a dab of glue at the bottom portion for each ear. Clip and let dry (see p. 74-point ③).

7 Apply a thin layer of glue on both sides of the paws with a bamboo stick and let dry. ▶ point ②

8 Cut the fingertips once the glue has dried. ▶ point ③

9 Determine the paw and ear placement (see p. 49) and attach with glue.

Trimming and Sizing Guide

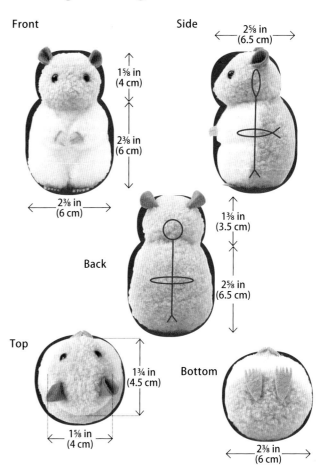

Front

Side — 2⅝ in (6.5 cm)

1⅝ in (4 cm)

2⅜ in (6 cm)

2⅜ in (6 cm)

Back

1⅜ in (3.5 cm)

2⅝ in (6.5 cm)

Top

1¾ in (4.5 cm)

1⅝ in (4 cm)

Bottom

2⅜ in (6 cm)

point ①

To make the arms and legs extend out, trim as shown in the photos.

point ②

For the front paws, lightly pinch each paw with your fingers before the glue dries to give them a rounded shape. Once the shape has taken hold, release and let fully dry.

point ③

Harden with glue first before cutting out the little fingertips. Apply another layer of glue to the fingertips to reinforce.

Template (actual size)

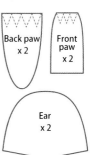

Back paw x 2

Front paw x 2

Ear x 2

Chick (see page 27)

(Template on page 94)

Winding Diagram
- Double strand
- [A] [B] same

String Knot (Back)
↓
[A] Front / [B] Back

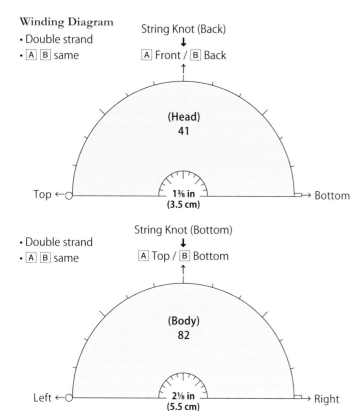

Top ←○   → Bottom

(Head) 41

1⅜ in (3.5 cm)

- Double strand
- [A] [B] same

String Knot (Bottom)
↓
[A] Top / [B] Bottom

Left ←○   → Right

(Body) 82

2⅛ in (5.5 cm)

Trimming and Sizing Guide

Front   Back   Side

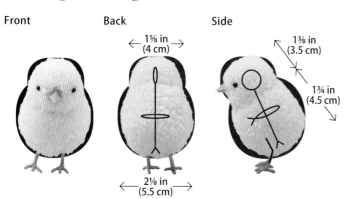

← 1⅝ in (4 cm) →

← 2⅛ in (5.5 cm) →

1⅜ in (3.5 cm)

1¾ in (4.5 cm)

Materials

Pom pom maker: Head: 1⅜ in (3.5 cm), Body: 2⅛ in (5.5 cm)
Yarn – sport weight in yellow

Other Materials
Eyes: plastic safety eye (black) 4 mm x 2
Beak: felt (yellow) 1⅛ x 1⅛ (3 x 3 cm)
Wire: (#24) 7 in (18 cm)
#25 Embroidery floss (beige) 1 skein

Instructions

1 Follow the winding diagram and make one 1⅜ in (3.5 cm) pom pom and one 2⅛ in (5.5 cm). Remove from pom pom maker and adjust shape.

2 Attach head to body (see p. 52-B). Cut out beak using template and apply a thin layer of glue on both sides with a bamboo stick. Fold the middle to form the beak and let dry (see p. 51).

3 Trim as shown in photos below.

4 Determine eye and beak placement and attach with glue (see p. 44).

5 Shape the wire as shown. Take three strands of embroidery floss. Add glue to the wire little by little and carefully wrap it with floss.
▶ point ①

6 Determine eye position and attach with glue (see p. 47–48). Then do the same with the nose. ▶ point ①

point ①

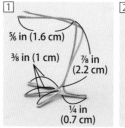

⅝ in (1.6 cm)

⅜ in (1 cm)   ⅞ in (2.2 cm)

¼ in (0.7 cm)

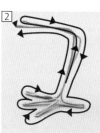

Shape the wire into the legs [1]. Follow the direction of the arrows to wrap the embroidery floss [2].

point ②

By attaching the legs somewhat towards the front of the body in a way that almost tilts it forward, balance is easier to achieve (see the photo on the left). Separate the yarn where the legs will be placed on the pom pom and add glue to both the pom pom and legs to attach.

Hamburger (see page 28)

(Template on page 93)

Winding Diagram

· Double strand for the bun
· Single strand for hamburger patty
· A B same

※Cut the light yellow felt into a square and cut out the center.

※See p. 43-2 for yarn winding instructions

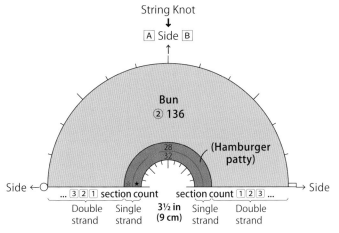

String Knot
↓
A Side B

Bun
② 136

(Hamburger patty)

28
32

Side ← ... ③②① section count   section count ①②③ ... → Side

| Double strand | Single strand | 3½ in (9 cm) | Single strand | Double strand |

Materials

Pom pom maker: 3½ in (9 cm)
Yarn – worsted weight in light brown and brown

Other Materials
Felt (red) 7 x 7 in (18 x 18 cm)
Felt (light yellow) 3⅜ x 3⅜ in (8.5 x 8.5 cm)
Felt (yellow green) 4 x 8 in (10 x 20 cm)

Instructions

1 Follow the winding diagram and make a 3½ in (9 cm) pom pom.
2 Remove from pom pom maker, adjust shape and trim as shown in photos. Check frequently from above as you trim that the shape looks evenly rounded.
3 Continue to round out the hamburger and use the stepped cut method (see p. 50).
4 Cut out the various felt elements using the templates. ▶ point ①
Glue three layers of the red felt before cutting. ▶ point ②
5 Insert the light yellow, red and yellow green felt pieces from step 4 (in that order) between the patty and bun. Attach the felt edges with glue. ▶ point ③

Trimming and Sizing Guide

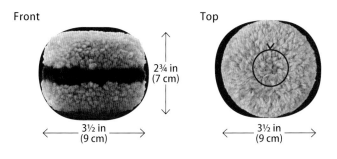

Front

2¾ in (7 cm)

3½ in (9 cm)

Top

3½ in (9 cm)

Top

1⅝ in (4 cm)

Bottom

2 in (5 cm)

point ①

Use the templates to cut out the felt pieces. Because these will be inserted into the pom pom, cut a slit on one side of each piece to make the placement easier.

point ②

Apply glue on the entire surface, layer three pieces and let dry. Once dry, use the template to cut out shape.

point ③

Spread the space between the burger and bun with a tool such as tweezers and insert the felt toppings. Secure the slit section of each felt layer into the pom pom with glue and make sure that they are positioned in the pom pom to hide the slits.

Broccoli (see page 28, 29)

Winding Diagram

- Double strand
- A B same

String Knot (Bottom)
↓
A Top / B Bottom

(Floret)
26

Left ←○

1⅜ in
(3.5 cm)

→ Right

- Double strand
- A B same

※ Wind the floret pom pom extra tightly

String Knot (Top)
↓
A Top / B Bottom

(Stem)
47

Left ←○

1⅜ in
(3.5 cm)

→ Right

Materials
Pom pom maker: Floret, stalk: 1⅜ in (3.5 cm)
Yarn – Floret: worsted weight in deep green
　　　Stalk: DK weight in light green

Instructions

1 Follow the winding diagram and make two 1⅜ in (3.5 cm) pom poms. Remove from pom pom maker and adjust shape.
2 Trim the stalk pom pom into a cylindrical shape. ▶ point ①
3 Use a felting needle on the pom pom from step 2 to hide the string. ▶ point ②
4 Trim to flatten the bottom of the pom pom from step 3. ▶ point ③
5 Position the floret pom pom with the string knot on the bottom and roughly trim as shown in the photos. Connect to the stalk pom pom from step 4 (see p. 52-A).

point ①

point ②

point ③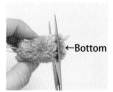

←Bottom

While keeping an eye on the string, trim to make each side of the stalk straight.

Hide the string by felting the yarn surrounding the string with a felting needle.

No need to trim the top since it will be connected to the floret.

Trimming and Sizing Guide

Front

Top

Bottom

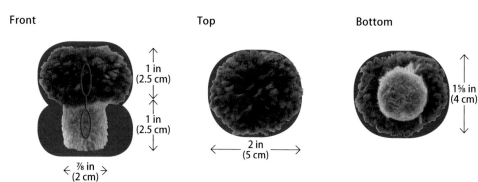

1 in
(2.5 cm)

1 in
(2.5 cm)

⅞ in
(2 cm)

2 in
(5 cm)

1⅝ in
(4 cm)

Apple (see page 29)

(Template on page 86)

Winding Diagram
- Double strand
- A B same

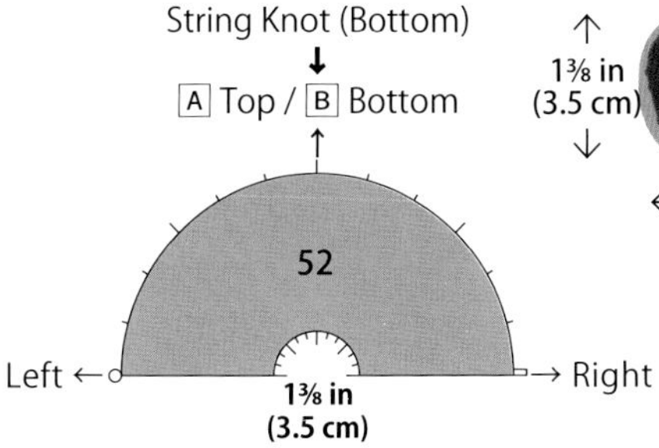

String Knot (Bottom)
↓
A Top / B Bottom
↑

52

Left ←○——————○→ Right

1⅜ in
(3.5 cm)

Trimming Guide

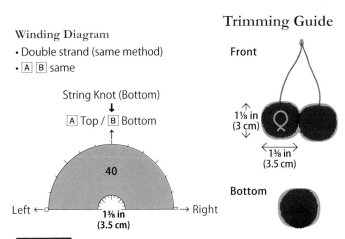

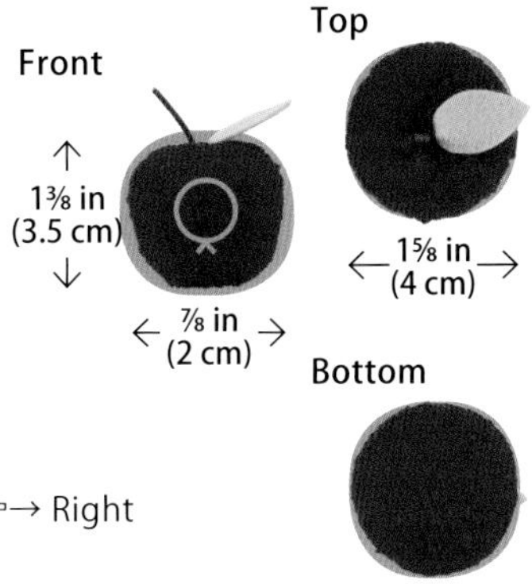

Front

↑
1⅜ in
(3.5 cm)
↓

← ⅞ in →
(2 cm)

Top

← 1⅝ in →
(4 cm)

Bottom

Materials
Pom pom maker: 1⅜ in (3.5 cm)
Yarn – machine washable merino worsted weight in red

Other Materials
Core: craft cord (brown) 2¾ in (7 cm)
Leaf: felt (yellow green) 1⅝ x 1⅛ in (4 x 3 cm)

Instructions

1 Follow the winding diagram and make a 1⅜ in (3.5 cm) pom pom. Remove from pom pom maker and adjust shape.
2 Using a yarn needle, insert the craft cord into the pom pom string loop and tie firmly to create the stem. Cut one end of the cord close to the knot and add a dab of glue on the knot to secure.
3 Trim the pom pom as shown in photo. ▶ **point** ① Trim to create an indentation around the cord stem. ▶ **point** ② Cut the string close to the knot.
4 Cut out the felt leaf using the template. Attach near the cord stem with glue.

point ①

point ②

Trim the sides at an angle with a slight concave curve.

Trim the area around the cord to create an indentation.

Cherry (see page 28)

Winding Diagram
- Double strand (same method)
- A B same

String Knot (Bottom)
↓
A Top / B Bottom
↑

40

Left ←○——————○→ Right

1⅜ in
(3.5 cm)

Trimming Guide

Front

↑
1⅛ in
(3 cm)
↓

← 1⅜ in →
(3.5 cm)

Bottom

Materials
Pom pom maker: 1⅜ in (3.5 cm)
Yarn – machine washable merino worsted weight in red

Other Materials
Craft cord (dark green) 8 in (20 cm)
#25 Embroidery floss (beige) 4 in (10 cm)

Instructions

1 Follow the winding diagram and make a 1⅜ in (3.5 cm) pom pom. Remove from pom pom maker and adjust shape.
2 Follow step 2 of the apple to attach cord to pom pom string. Cut one end of cord.
3 Trim into a round shape as shown in the photos. ▶ **point** ①
4 Repeat steps 1–3 with a second pom pom. Glue the ends of the cords together and wrap with embroidery thread. ▶ **point** ②

point ①

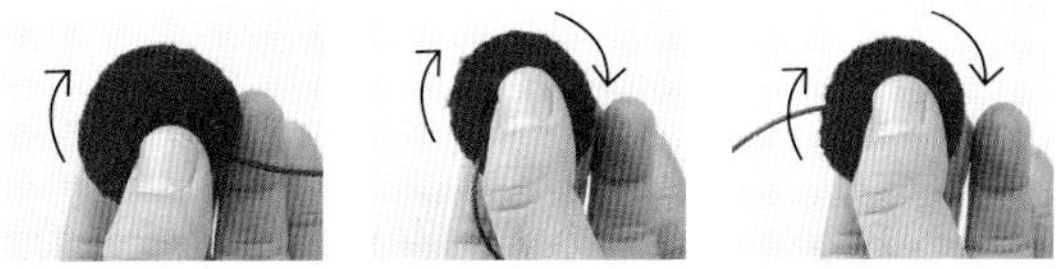

Place your finger in the center of the pom pom and without moving your finger, slowly trim around the pom pom to form a circular shape.

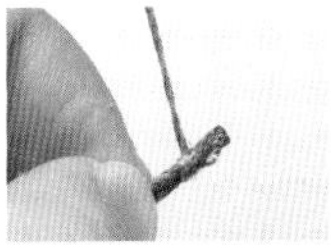

point ②

When attaching the cord ends, add a little glue and then wrap with embroidery floss. Add a dab of glue to secure the floss when you've finished wrapping.

Rice Ball (Onigiri) 2 types umeboshi (pickled plum) • seaweed (see page 29)

(see page 29)

Materials

Pom pom maker: 2⅛ in (5.5 cm)
Yarn – Seaweed onigiri / washable sport weight in off-white
   Umeboshi [Pickled plum] onigiri / rice: machine washable sport weight in off-white
   Umeboshi [Pickled plum]: machine washable merino worsted weight in red

Other Materials
Seaweed: felt (black) 3½ x 1 in (8.9 x 2.5 cm)
Umeboshi [pickled plum]: felt (black) 8⅜ x 1⅜ in (21.2 x 3.5 cm)

Instructions (same method)

1 Follow the winding diagram and make a 2⅛ in (5.5 cm) pom pom.
2 Remove from pom pom maker, adjust shape and cut string as close to the knot as possible. Trim to create a triangle with rounded corners.
3 Trim to flatten the front and back as shown in the photos below.
4 Cut the felt using dimensions provided. Attach to the pom pom with glue.

Trimming Guide

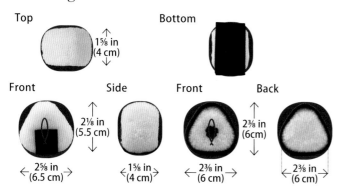

Top

1⅝ in (4 cm)

Bottom

Front   Side   Front   Back

2⅛ in (5.5 cm)   2⅜ in (6cm)

← 2⅝ in (6.5 cm) →   ← 1⅝ in (4 cm) →   ← 2⅜ in (6 cm) →   ← 2⅜ in (6 cm) →

Sausage (see page 29)

(see page 29)

Materials

Pom pom maker: 1⅜ in (3.5 cm)
Yarn – machine washable sport weight in reddish brown
   Cut marks Sausage: pom pom yarn in pale warm brown

Instructions (same method)

1 Follow the winding diagram (see p. 81) and make two 1⅜ in (3.5 cm) pom poms.
2 Remove from pom pom maker and adjust shape.
3 Connect the pom poms (see p. 52). Cut the string close to the knot.
4 Use a felting needle to blend where the two pom poms connect.
▶ point ① Trim as shown in the photos on page 81. ▶ point ①
5 Place the pale warm brown yarn strand at an angle in the middle of the pom pom from step 4. Use the felting needle to felt the yarn into the pom pom to create a "cut mark". Once felted, cut the yarn. Repeat with three other cut marks. ▶ point ②

point ①   point ②

Lightly felt the yarn with the needle

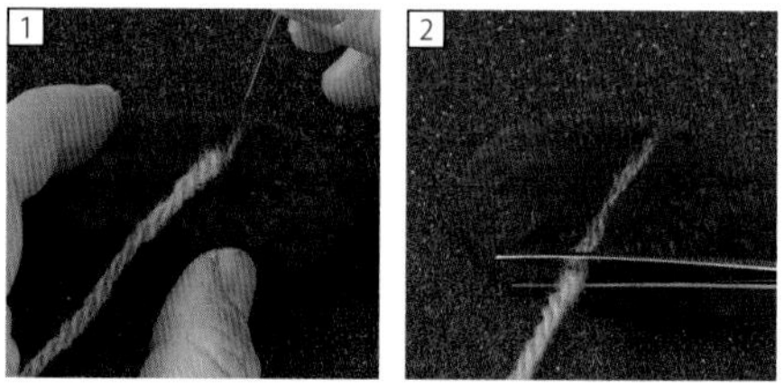

Once the yarn adheres to the pom pom, cut the yarn and blend in further with the felting needle.

Pickled plum (Umeboshi)
· Single strand for red in section ①
· Double strand for white in sections ②③④

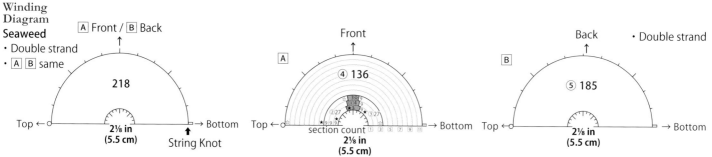

Winding Diagram
Seaweed
· Double strand
· Ⓐ Ⓑ same

Ⓐ Front / Ⓑ Back

218

Top ←○   2⅛ in (5.5 cm)   → Bottom

String Knot

Front

Ⓐ   ④ 136

②27   ③27

section count ① ③ ⑤ ⑦ ⑨ ⑪
Top ←○   2⅛ in (5.5 cm)   → Bottom

Back   · Double strand

Ⓑ   ⑤ 185

Top ←○   2⅛ in (5.5 cm)   → Bottom

Fried Shrimp (see page 29)

(Template on page 93)

Winding Diagram

- Double strand
- A B same

String Knot (Bottom)
↓
A Top / B Bottom

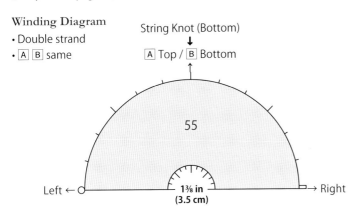

55

Left ← O   1⅜ in (3.5 cm)   → Right

Materials

Pom pom maker 1⅜ in (3.5 cm)
Yarn – machine washable merino worsted weight in yellow

Other Materials
Wire (#20) Approximately 8 in (20 cm)
Tail: felt (red) 2⅜ x 1⅝ in (6 x 4 cm)

Instructions

1 Follow the winding diagram and make four 1⅜ in (3.5cm) pom poms. Remove from pom pom maker and adjust shape. Connect with the wire. ▶ point ①

2 Trim and round out the shape as shown in the photos below.

3 Spread out the yarn on the thinner end. Reinforce the felt piece by applying a thin layer of glue on both sides (see p. 51). Once dry, cut out using the template and attach to the pom pom with glue.

Trimming Guide

Front   **Back**

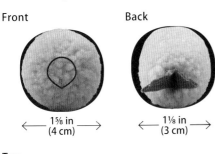

← 1⅝ in (4 cm) →   ← 1⅛ in (3 cm) →

Top

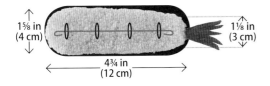

↑ 1⅝ in (4 cm) ↓   ↑ 1⅛ in (3 cm) ↓

← 4¾ in (12 cm) →

point ①

1

Bend one end of the wire to form a hook

2

Insert the wire through one pom pom, hooking the curved end of the wire on the string in the center of the pom pom. Add a dab of glue to secure the hook. Add more glue along the length of the wire and add the other three pom poms onto the wire.

3

When the last pom pom has been added, push the pom poms together and bend the other end of the wire. Use wire cutters to cut off the extra wire, then curl the newly shortened end into the last pom pom. Secure with glue.

Sausage Trimming Guide

Top   **Side**

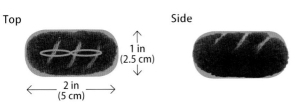

← 2 in (5 cm) →   ↑ 1 in (2.5 cm) ↓

Winding Diagram

- Double strand
- A B same

String Knot (Left)
↓
A Right / B Left

47

Top ← O   1⅜ in (3.5 cm)   → Bottom

Boiled Egg (see page 28)

Winding Diagram

- Single strand of lemon for section ①
- Double strand of off-white for sections ② ③

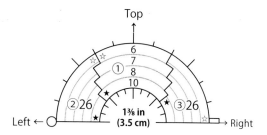

Top

6
7
① 8
10
② 26   ③ 26
1⅜ in
(3.5 cm)
Left ←   → Right

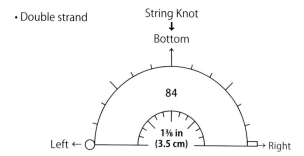

- Double strand

String Knot
↓
Bottom

84

1⅜ in
(3.5 cm)
Left ←   → Right

Trimming and Sizing Guide

Front

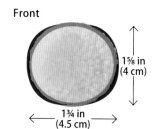

1⅝ in
(4 cm)

1¾ in
(4.5 cm)

Back

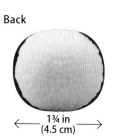

1¾ in
(4.5 cm)

Side

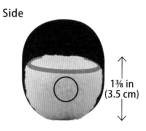

1⅜ in
(3.5 cm)

Materials

Pom pom maker 1⅜ in (3.5 cm)
Yarn – Egg white: machine washable sport weight in off-white
          Yolk: worsted weight in lemon

Instructions

1 Follow the winding diagram and make one 1⅜ in (3.5 cm). ▶ point ①
2 Remove from pom pom maker, adjust the shape and trim into an egg shape as shown in the photos below.
3 Rearrange the yarn for the yolk and shape it into a circle.
4 Use the felting needle to lightly stab the edge of the egg white section; this prevents the yarn from rising up unevenly.

point ①

Wind the yellow yarn in the center section and try not to distribute the yarn across the pom pom maker arm. This will make the yolk appear rounder.

point ②

Wind the white yarn in the outer sections, making sure that no yarn is caught in the pom pom maker closure.

Winding complete

Round Cake (see page 30)

Winding Diagram
- Single strand for all
- A B same

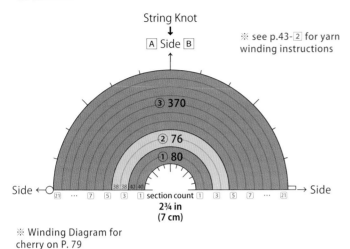

String Knot
↓
A Side B

※ see p.43-2 for yarn winding instructions

③ 370
② 76
① 80

Side ← ⟶ Side

38 38 40 40

21 ... 7 5 3 1 section count 1 3 5 7 ... 21

2¾ in
(7 cm)

※ Winding Diagram for cherry on P. 79

Materials
Pom pom maker: Cherry: 1⅜ in (3.5 cm), Cake: 2¾ in (7 cm)
Yarn – Cake layers: machine washable sport weight in dark brown
    Frosting: machine washable sport weight in pinl
    Cherry: machine washable merino worsted weight in red

Other Materials
Cherry stem: craft cord (deep green) 4 in (10 cm)

Instructions
1 Follow the winding diagram and make one 2¾ in (7 cm) pom pom.
2 Remove from pom pom maker, adjust the yarn with tweezers, then cut the string near the knot.
3 Hold the pom pom so that the pink frosting is vertical, and trim to straighten the sides. ▶ point ①
4 Then tip the pom pom so that the pink frosting is now horizontal and trim to straighten the top and bottom. Keep checking from above as you trim, making sure the cake looks round. Lightly felt the side of the cake with a needle to prevent yarn from loosening.
5 Make the cherry (see p. 79).
6 Attach the cherry from step 5 on top of the cake with glue.

Trimming and Sizing Guide

Front

Top

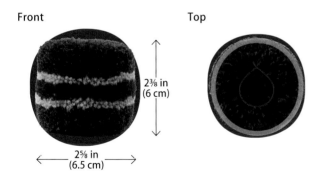

2⅜ in
(6 cm)

2⅝ in
(6.5 cm)

point ①

Trim to straighten the sides.

point ②

Trim to straighten the top and bottom (the cherry will go on top).

Cupcake (see page 31)

Winding Diagram

• Double strand (frosting 1 and 2 are the same)

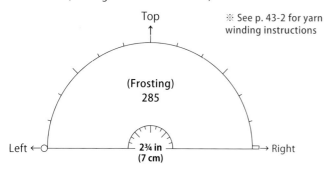

Top

※ See p. 43-2 for yarn winding instructions

(Frosting)
285

Left ← ○

2¾ in
(7 cm)

→ Right

String Knot
↓
Bottom

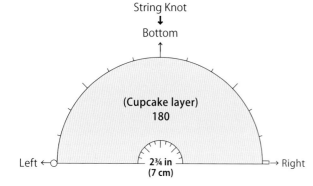

(Cupcake layer)
180

Left ← ○

2¾ in
(7 cm)

→ Right

※ Winding diagram for the strawberry is the same as the cherry on p. 79. Tie the string at the bottom.

Materials

Pom pom maker: Strawberry: 1⅜ in (3.5 cm), Cupcake: 2¾ in (7 cm)
Yarn – Cupcake layer: machine washable merino worsted weight in yellow
Frosting 1: machine washable sport weight in off-white
Frosting 2: machine washable sport weight in pink
Strawberry: machine washable merino worsted weight in red

Instructions

1 Follow the winding diagram for the cupcake layer and make a 2¾ in (7 cm) pom pom. Remove from the pom pom maker, adjust the shape and cut the string close to the knot.

2 Use the stepped cut method where the cupcake layer meets the frosting portion (see p. 50).

3 Trim the cupcake layer as shown in the photos blow. ▶ point ①

4 Trim to round out the frosting portion, checking frequently from above as you trim.

5 Make a 1⅜ in (3.5 cm) pom pom with the yarn specified for the strawberry. Trim into a strawberry shape as shown in the photos below.

6 Attach the strawberry from step 5 on top of the cupcake with glue.

point ①

Trim the cupcake layer so the frosting is wider. Keep checking while trimming the frosting to make it uniformly rounded. Flatten the bottom of the cupcake layer.

Trimming and Sizing Guide

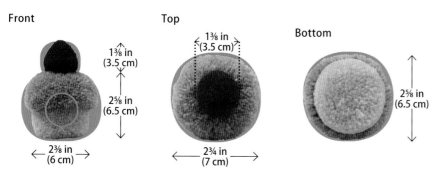

Front

1⅜ in
(3.5 cm)

2⅝ in
(6.5 cm)

← 2⅜ in (6 cm) →

Top

1⅜ in
(3.5 cm)

← 2¾ in (7 cm) →

Bottom

2⅝ in
(6.5 cm)

Ice Cream Cones (see page 32)

(Template on page 93)

Winding Diagram
- Single strand
- A B same

String Knot (Bottom)
↓
A Top / B Bottom

75

Side ←○

1⅜ in
(3.5 cm)

Side

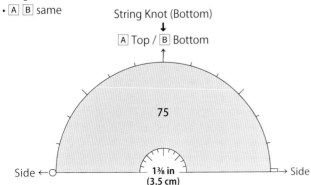

Trimming and Sizing Guide

Front

Front

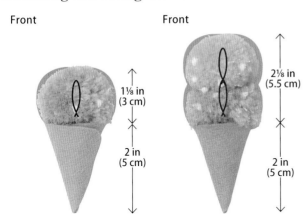

1⅛ in
(3 cm)

2 in
(5 cm)

2⅛ in
(5.5 cm)

2 in
(5 cm)

Top

Bottom

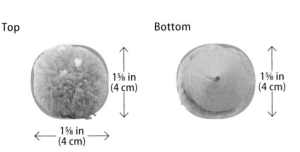

1⅝ in
(4 cm)

1⅝ in
(4 cm)

1⅝ in
(4 cm)

Materials
Pom pom maker: 1⅜ in (3.5 cm)
Yarn – Single scoop: DK weight in pink and white
            Double scoop: DK weight in pale orange and pale blue

Other Materials
Cone: felt (ocher) 2¾ x 4⅜ in (7 x 11 cm), cotton batting as needed

Instructions (same for both)

1 Follow the winding diagram and make 1⅜ in (3.5cm) pom pom. For a single scoop, make one pom pom; for a double scoop, make two pom poms.
2 Remove from pom pom maker, adjust the shape and trim to an evenly round shape. Cut the string close to the knot (for the double scoop, don't cut the string).
3 For the double scoop, connect the two pom poms (see p. 52-A).
4 Make the cone. Cut the shape out using the template. Add glue on edge as indicated, and using tweezers, roll the felt into a cone-shape. ▶ point ①
5 Add glue inside the cone from step 4, and leaving about ¼ in (5 mm) from the top edge, fill with cotton batting. Add glue to the top of the batting, the outer and inner edges of the cone, and attach pom pom. ▶ point ②

point ①

Transfer the ★ markings from the template onto the felt. Add glue to the felt and using tweezers to hold down the edge, fold/roll the felt to match up the markings.

Roll to form a cone-shape and glue together.

point ②

Add glue to the batting, outer and inner edges of the cone to ensure that the ice cream scoop is solidly attached to the cone.

Apple Pencil Topper (see page 33)

Winding Diagram

- Double strand
- Ⓐ Ⓑ same

String Knot
↓
Ⓐ Side Ⓑ

65

Side ←○　2⅛ in　□→ Side
(5.5 cm)

Template (actual size)
(Same as apple on p. 75)

(Leaf)

Trimming and Sizing Guide

Front

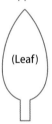

1⅜ in
(3.5 cm)

← 1⅜ in →
(3.5 cm)

Top

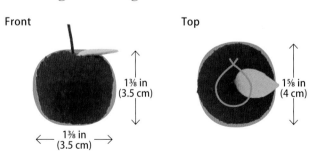

1⅝ in
(4 cm)

Materials

Pom pom maker: 2⅛ in (5.5 cm)
Yarn – machine washable merino worsted weight in red

Other Materials
Leaf: felt (yellow green) 1⅝ x 1 in (4 x 2.5 cm)
Stem: Decorative cord (brown) 2 in (5 cm)
Pencil

Instructions

1 Follow the winding diagram and make a 2⅛ in (5.5 cm) pom pom. Place the pencil in the center of the pom pom maker and tie the pom pom onto the pencil. ▶ point ①

2 Remove from the pom pom maker and adjust the shape. Insert the cord into the center and attach to the pencil with glue. ▶ point ②
Spread out the yarn at the base of the apple. Add glue and attach the surrounding yarn to the pencil. Trim as shown in the photos below and cut the cord to your liking.

3 Cut out felt using template and attach to the base of the cord with glue.

point ①

Tie the string around the pencil as well. When removing from the pom pom arm, make sure the pencil doesn't fall out.

point ②

Insert the cord and attach to the eraser with glue.

New Year's Rice Cakes (*Kagami Mochi*)   (see page 34)

Winding Diagram
- Single strand
- A B same

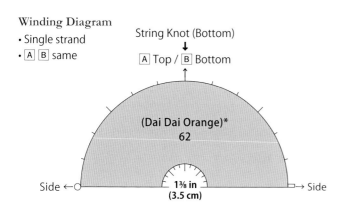

String Knot (Bottom)
↓
A Top / B Bottom

(Dai Dai Orange)*
62

Side ←○
1⅜ in
(3.5 cm)
→ Side

- Double strand
- A B same

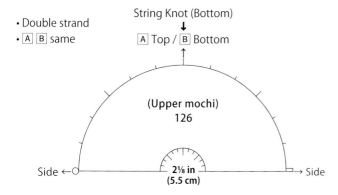

String Knot (Bottom)
↓
A Top / B Bottom

(Upper mochi)
126

Side ←○
2⅛ in
(5.5 cm)
→ Side

- Double strand
- A B same

※ See p. 43-2 for yarn winding instructions.

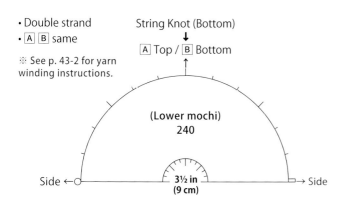

String Knot (Bottom)
↓
A Top / B Bottom

(Lower mochi)
240

Side ←○
3½ in
(9 cm)
→ Side

* a Japanese bitter orange

Materials

Pom pom maker: Dai Dai Orange: 1⅜ in (3.5 cm)
  Mochi: 2⅛ in (5.5 cm), 3½ in (9 cm)
Yarn – Dai Dai Orange: worsted weight in orange
  Mochi: machine washable worsted weight in white

Other Materials
Leaf: felt (yellow green) ⅞ x 1⅝ in (2 x 4 cm)

Instructions (same for both)

1 Follow the winding diagram and make one 1⅜ in (3.5 cm), one 2⅛ in (5.5 cm) pom pom and one 3½ in (9 cm) pom pom. Remove from pom pom maker, adjust shape and trim as shown in photos below.
2 Connect in this order: Dai Dai orange, first mochi (2⅛ in [5.5 cm]), second mochi (3½ in [9 cm]) (see p. 52-A). ▶ point ①
3 Cut out felt using template and attach leaf to the Dai Dai Orange with glue.

point ①

When attaching the orange to the first mochi (2⅛ in [5.5 cm]), use a yarn needle. Then attach the larger mochi (3½ in [9 cm]) by pulling the string through with a crochet hook.

Trimming and Sizing Guide

Front   Top

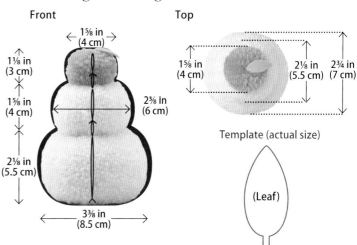

Front:
← 1⅝ in (4 cm) →
1⅛ in (3 cm)
1⅝ in (4 cm)
2⅜ in (6 cm)
2⅛ in (5.5 cm)
3⅜ in (8.5 cm)

Top:
1⅝ in (4 cm)
2⅛ in (5.5 cm)
2¾ in (7 cm)

Template (actual size)

(Leaf)

87

Two Types of Flowers (see page 35)

(Pentagon shape guide page 95)

Winding Diagram

- Single strand
- A B same

String Knot
↓
A Side B

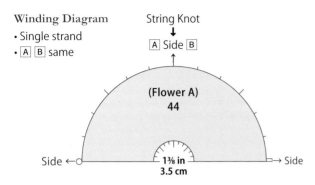

(Flower A)
44

Side ←o   1⅜ in
3.5 cm   → Side

- Single strand
- A B same

String Knot
↓
A Side B

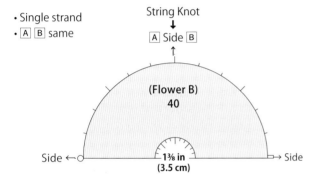

(Flower B)
40

Side ←o   1⅜ in
(3.5 cm)   → Side

Trimming and Sizing Guide

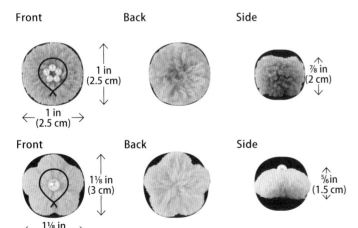

Front   Back   Side

1 in (2.5 cm)   ⅞ in (2 cm)

← 1 in (2.5 cm) →

Front   Back   Side

1⅛ in (3 cm)   ⅝ in (1.5 cm)

← 1⅛ in (3 cm) →

Materials

Pom pom maker: 1⅜ in (3.5 cm)
Yarn – Flower A: machine washable sport weight in yellow green, blue and/or light blue
    Flower B: pom pom yarn in white and/or pink

Other Materials
Flower A / pearl beads 3 mm x 5, beading thread 4¾ in (12 cm)
Flower B / pearl beads ¼ in (6 mm)

Instructions (Flower A)

1 Follow the winding diagram and make one 1⅜ in (3.5 cm) pom pom. Remove from pom pom maker and adjust shape. Cut the string close to the knot.
2 Add a dab of glue along the center string loop holding the pom pom together and attach the surrounding yarn to the glue to hide the string. Trim as shown in photos below.
3 String the beads onto the beading thread and make the flower center. ▶ point ①
4 Glue the beads from step 3 in the middle of the flower (if you prefer, feel free to glue on additional beads).

Instructions (Flower B)

1 Follow the winding diagram and make one 1⅜ in (3.5cm) pom pom. Remove from pom pom maker and adjust shape. Cut the string close to the knot.
2 Felt the area in and around the center string with a needle.
3 Felt the lines into the petal portions. ▶ point ② Cut into 5 petal shapes.
4 Attach the beads to the center of the flower with glue.

point ①

point ②

String the beads onto beading thread, form a ring and tie firmly. Add a dab of glue on the knot. Thread one end of the beading thread into the closest bead and hide the knot. Once the glue is dry, cut the beading thread.

Use the pentagon shaped guide (see p. 95) to felt the lines into the flower petals.

Heart (see page 34)

Winding Diagram
- Double strand
- A B same

※ Double strand for the pink color, wind 102 times

String Knot (Back)
A Front / B Back

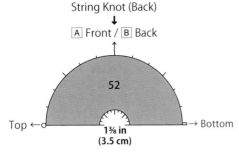

52

Top ← | → Bottom

1⅜ in (3.5 cm)

Materials
Pom pom maker: 1⅜ in (3.5 cm)
Yarn – machine washable worsted weight in red and/or fingering yarn in soft pink

Instructions (same for both)

1 Follow the winding diagram and make a 1⅜ in (3.5 cm) pom pom. Remove from pom pom and adjust shape.
2 Trim as shown in photos below. ▶ point ①

point ①

Trim into a heart shape. Create an indentation between the two rounded tops and lightly felt it with a needle. This will maintain the shape.

Trimming Guide

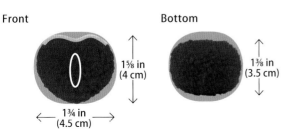

Front

Bottom

1⅝ in (4 cm)

1⅜ in (3.5 cm)

1¾ in (4.5 cm)

Snow Rabbit (see page 34)

(Template on page 95)

Winding Diagram
- Double strand
- A B same

String Knot (Bottom)
A Top / B Bottom

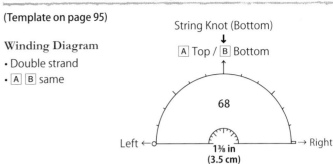

68

Left ← | → Right

1⅜ in (3.5 cm)

Materials
Pom pom maker: 1⅜ in (3.5 cm)
Yarn – pom pom yarn in white

Other Materials
Eyes: plastic safety eye (red) 4 mm x 2
Ears: felt (yellow green) ⅞ x ⅞ in (2 x 2 cm) x 2

Instructions

1 Follow the winding diagram and make a 1⅜ in (3.5 cm) pom pom. Remove from pom pom maker and adjust shape.
2 Trim into a rather elliptical shape as shown in photo below. Trim to flatten the bottom.
3 Determine eye placement and attach with glue (see p. 44).
4 Cut out felt using template, determine ear placement and attach with glue. ▶ point ①

point ①
Attach ears so they angle outward a little

Trimming Guide

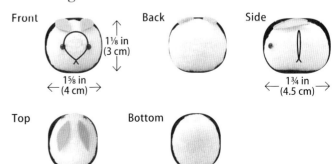

Front

Back

Side

1⅛ in (3 cm)

1⅝ in (4 cm)

1¾ in (4.5 cm)

Top

Bottom

89

Halloween Pumpkin (see page 35)

Winding Diagram
- Double strand
- A B same

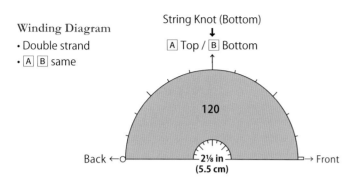

String Knot (Bottom)

A Top / B Bottom

120

Back ← Front

2⅛ in
(5.5 cm)

Materials

Pom pom maker: 2⅛ in (5.5 cm)
Yarn – machine washable merino worsted weightin orange

Other Materials
Stem: felt (deep green) 1¾ x 1¾ in (4.5 x 4.5 cm)
Eyes, nose, mouth: felt (black) 2⅜ x 1⅝ in (6 x 4 cm)

Instructions

1 Follow winding diagram and make a 2⅛ in (5.5 cm) pom pom. Remove from pom pom maker and adjust shape.

2 Trim as shown in photos on left. ▶ point ①

3 Cut out felt using templates. Attach eyes, nose and mouth with glue.

4 For the stem, cut three ⅜ x 1⅛ in (1 x 3 cm) pieces of green felt and glue all three layers together. Once the glue is dry, cut into a horn-shape and roll into a cylinder. Attach to the top of the pumpkin with glue.

Trimming and Sizing Guide

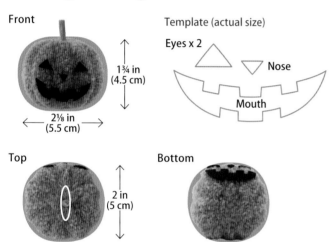

Front

1¾ in
(4.5 cm)

2⅛ in
(5.5 cm)

Top

2 in
(5 cm)

Bottom

Template (actual size)

Eyes x 2

Nose

Mouth

point ①

Mark the stem placement with a pin. Hold the pom pom so the center string is horizontal and trim the yarn along the string to create a ridge. Rotate the string 36 degrees (or 1/10th of the pom pom) and trim another ridge. Repeat this five times to create the ribs on the pumpkin shell.

Winding Diagram

Calico Cat
- Single strand for all

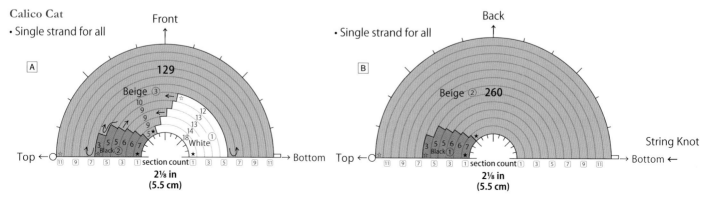

A

129

Beige ③

10
9
9
5

12
13
13
14
18
White ①

3 5 5 6 6 7
Black ②

Top ← ⑪ ⑨ ⑦ ⑤ ③ ① section count ① ③ ⑤ ⑦ ⑨ ⑪ → Bottom

2⅛ in
(5.5 cm)

- Single strand for all

B

Back

Beige ② 260

3 5 5 6 6 7
Black ①

String Knot

Top ← ⑪ ⑨ ⑦ ⑤ ③ ① section count ① ③ ⑤ ⑦ ⑨ ⑪ → Bottom ←

2⅛ in
(5.5 cm)

Brown Tiger Cat

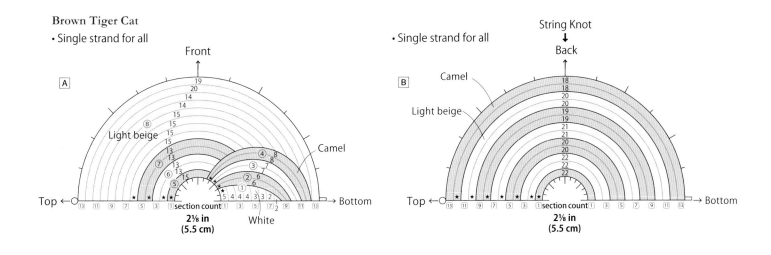

- Single strand for all

A

Front

19
20
14
15
⑧
15
Light beige
15
13
⑦
13
13
⑥
15
④ 8
⑤
③ 8
7
② 6
① 6

Camel

Top ← | ⑬ | ⑪ | ⑨ | ⑦ | ⑤ | ③ | ① section count ① | ③ | ⑤ | ⑦ | ⑨ | ⑪ | ⑬ | → Bottom
5 4 4 4 3 2

2⅛ in
(5.5 cm)

White

- Single strand for all

String Knot
↓
Back

B

Camel

Light beige

18
18
20
20
19
19
21
21
20
22
22
22

Top ← | ⑬ | ⑪ | ⑨ | ⑦ | ⑤ | ③ | ① section count ① | ③ | ⑤ | ⑦ | ⑨ | ⑪ | ⑬ | → Bottom

2⅛ in
(5.5 cm)

Penguin

(Head)

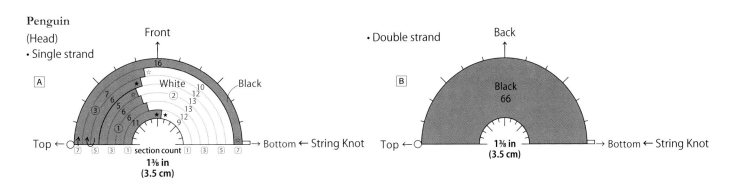

- Single strand

A

Front

16
☆
White
10
7
12
6
③ 6 13
② 13
6 12
① 11
9
★★
☆

Black

Top ← | ⑦ | ⑤ | ③ | ① section count ① | ③ | ⑤ | ⑦ | → Bottom ← String Knot

1⅜ in
(3.5 cm)

- Double strand

B

Back

Black
66

Top ← | → Bottom ← String Knot

1⅜ in
(3.5 cm)

(Body)

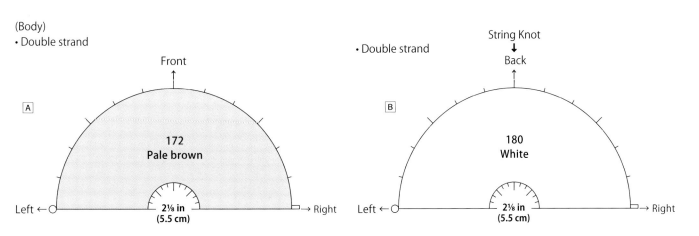

- Double strand

A

Front

172
Pale brown

Left ← | → Right

2⅛ in
(5.5 cm)

- Double strand

String Knot
↓
Back

B

180
White

Left ← | → Right

2⅛ in
(5.5 cm)

Miniature Schnauzer
(Head)
- Double strand of gray for sections ③～⑥
- Single strand of white for sections ① ②

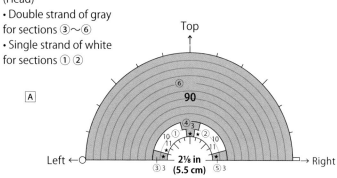

A

Top

90

⑥
④ 3
① ① ★ ② ⑩
⑩ ★ ⑩
⑪ ★ ⑪
★ ★
③ 3 **2⅛ in** ⑤ 3
(5.5 cm)

Left ← ○ ○ → Right

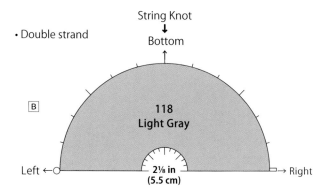

- Double strand

String Knot
↓
Bottom

B

118
Light Gray

2⅛ in
(5.5 cm)

Left ← ○ □ → Right

Hamster
- Double strand
- A B Same

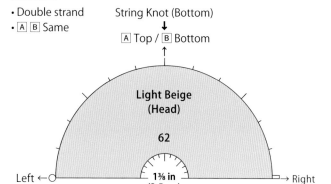

String Knot (Bottom)
↓
A Top / B Bottom

Light Beige
(Head)

62

1⅜ in
(3.5 cm)

Left ← ○ □ → Right

- Double strand
- A B Same

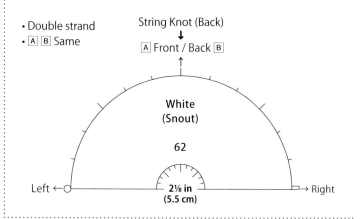

String Knot (Back)
↓
A Front / Back B

White
(Snout)

62

2⅛ in
(5.5 cm)

Left ← ○ □ → Right

- Double strand

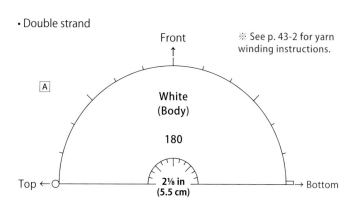

Front

※ See p. 43-2 for yarn winding instructions.

A

White
(Body)

180

2⅛ in
(5.5 cm)

Top ← ○ □ → Bottom

- Double strand

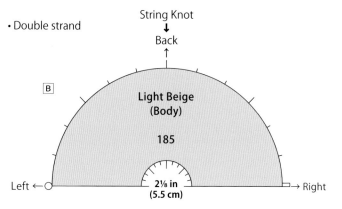

String Knot
↓
Back

B

Light Beige
(Body)

185

2⅛ in
(5.5 cm)

Left ← ○ □ → Right

Templates (actual size)

Templates for parts such as ears and
mouths to be made from wool roving
and felt.

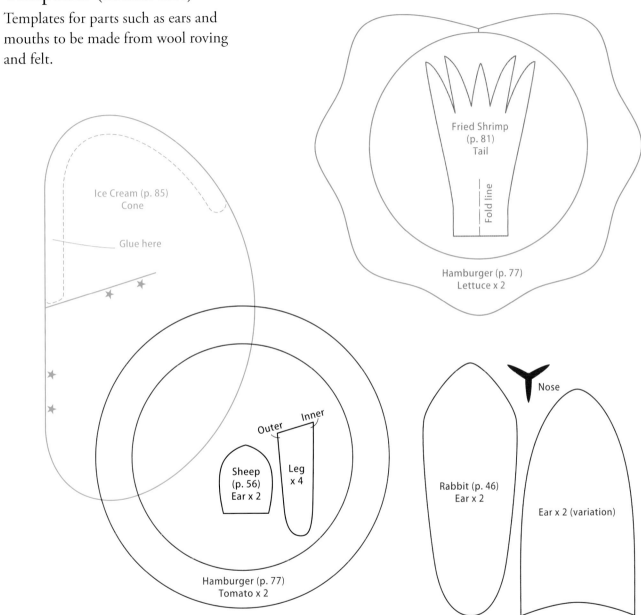

Fried Shrimp
(p. 81)
Tail

Fold line

Hamburger (p. 77)
Lettuce x 2

Ice Cream (p. 85)
Cone

Glue here

Outer   Inner

Sheep
(p. 56)
Ear x 2

Leg
x 4

Hamburger (p. 77)
Tomato x 2

Nose

Rabbit (p. 46)
Ear x 2

Ear x 2 (variation)

Cut cheese (light yellow) into a
7½ x 7½ in (19 x 19 cm) square
and use the tomato template
to cut out the center circle.

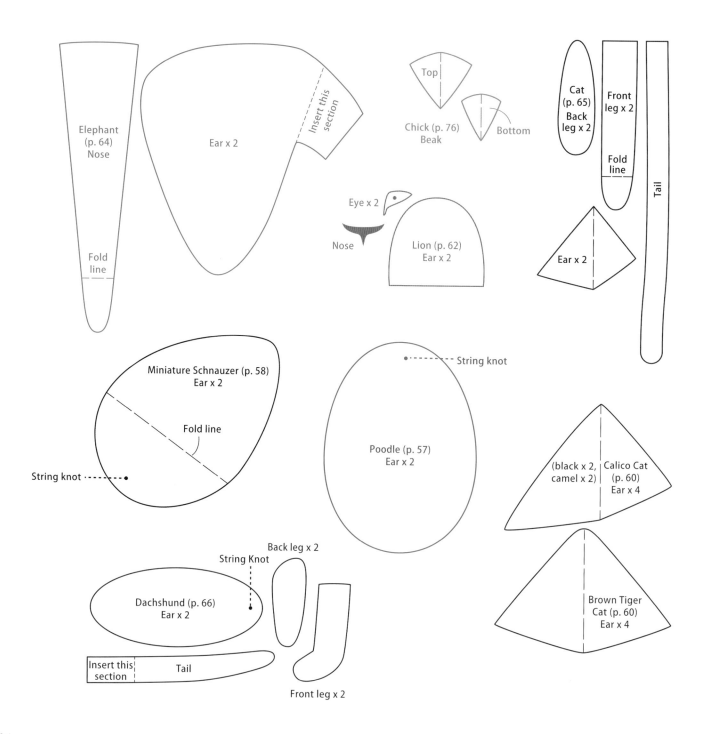

Elephant (p. 64) Nose

Fold line

Ear x 2

Insert this section

Top

Chick (p. 76) Beak

Bottom

Eye x 2

Nose

Lion (p. 62) Ear x 2

Cat (p. 65) Back leg x 2

Front leg x 2

Fold line

Tail

Ear x 2

Miniature Schnauzer (p. 58) Ear x 2

Fold line

String knot

String knot

Poodle (p. 57) Ear x 2

(black x 2, camel x 2)

Calico Cat (p. 60) Ear x 4

Brown Tiger Cat (p. 60) Ear x 4

Back leg x 2

String Knot

Dachshund (p. 66) Ear x 2

Insert this section

Tail

Front leg x 2

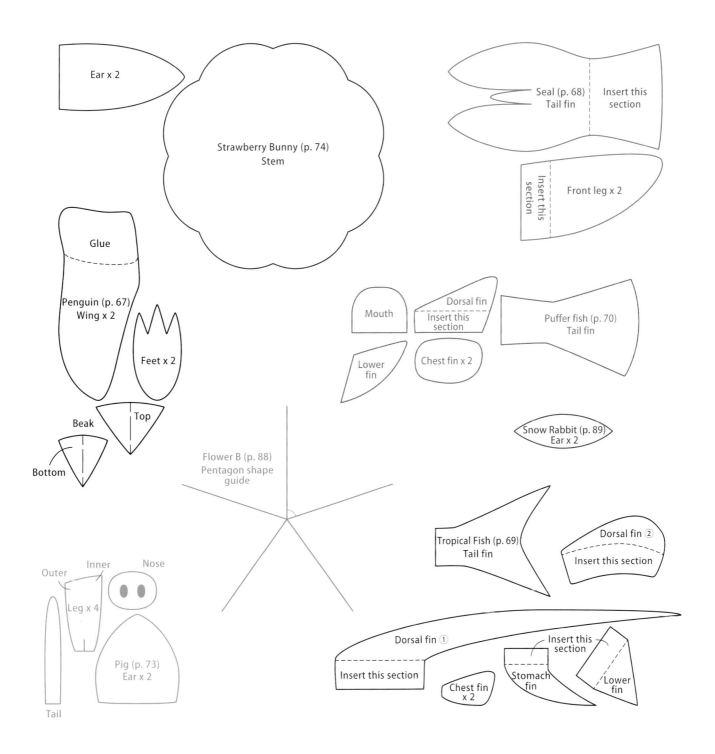

Ear x 2

Strawberry Bunny (p. 74)
Stem

Seal (p. 68)
Tail fin

Insert this section

Insert this section

Front leg x 2

Glue

Penguin (p. 67)
Wing x 2

Feet x 2

Beak

Top

Bottom

Mouth

Dorsal fin

Insert this section

Puffer fish (p. 70)
Tail fin

Lower fin

Chest fin x 2

Snow Rabbit (p. 89)
Ear x 2

Flower B (p. 88)
Pentagon shape guide

Tropical Fish (p. 69)
Tail fin

Dorsal fin ②

Insert this section

Outer

Inner

Nose

Leg x 4

Pig (p. 73)
Ear x 2

Tail

Dorsal fin ①

Insert this section

Chest fin x 2

Insert this section

Stomach fin

Lower fin

Published by Tuttle Publishing, an imprint of
Periplus Editions (HK) Ltd

www.tuttlepublishing.com

ISBN: 978-4-8053-1485-2

Pom Pom de Tsukuru Dobutsu to Motif by Kazuko Ito
© Kazuko Ito 2017

English translation rights arranged with
NIHONBUNGEISHA Co., Ltd., through Japan UNI Agency, Inc., Tokyo

English Translation ©2017 Periplus Editions (HK) Ltd
Translated from Japanese by Sanae Ishida
All rights reserved. No part of this publication
may be reproduced or utilized in any form or by
any means, electronic or mechanical, including photocopying,
recording, or by any information storage and retrieval system,
without prior written permission from the publisher.

Original Japanese edition
Photography: Norihito Amano (NIHONBUNGEISHA)
Styling: Akiko Suzuki
Model: Yumi Ito, Hiroki Ito
Design: Motoko Kitsukawa
Design Production: WADE
Editing: OMEGASHA
Supplies: FUJIKYU

Distributed by
North America, Latin America & Europe
Tuttle Publishing
364 Innovation Drive
North Clarendon, VT 05759-9436 U.S.A.
Tel: 1 (802) 773-8930; Fax: 1 (802) 773-6993
info@tuttlepublishing.com
www.tuttlepublishing.com

Japan
Tuttle Publishing
Yaekari Building, 3rd Floor
5-4-12 Osaki Shinagawa-ku, Tokyo 141-0032
Tel: (81) 3 5437-0171; Fax: (81) 3 5437-0755
sales@tuttle.co.jp
www.tuttle.co.jp

Asia Pacific
Berkeley Books Pte. Ltd.
61 Tai Seng Avenue, #02-12
Singapore 534167
Tel: (65) 6280-1330; Fax: (65) 6280-6290
inquiries@periplus.com.sg
www.periplus.com

20 19 18
10 9 8 7 6 5 4 3 2 1

Printed in China   1804RR

TUTTLE PUBLISHING® is a registered trademark of Tuttle Publishing,
a division of Periplus Editions (HK) Ltd.

About Tuttle
"Books to Span the East and West"

Our core mission at Tuttle Publishing is to create books which bring people together one page at a time. Tuttle was founded in 1832 in the small New England town of Rutland, Vermont (USA). Our fundamental values remain as strong today as they were then—to publish best-in-class books informing the English-speaking world about the countries and peoples of Asia. The world has become a smaller place today and Asia's economic, cultural and political influence has expanded, yet the need for meaningful dialogue and information about this diverse region has never been greater. Since 1948, Tuttle has been a leader in publishing books on the cultures, arts, cuisines, languages and literatures of Asia. Our authors and photographers have won numerous awards and Tuttle has published thousands of books on subjects ranging from martial arts to paper crafts. We welcome you to explore the wealth of information available on Asia at **www.tuttlepublishing.com.**